CONUNDRUM

THE EVOLUTION OF HOMOSEXUALITY

by
N. J. Peters

authorHOUSE™

1663 LIBERTY DRIVE, SUITE 200
BLOOMINGTON, INDIANA 47403
(800) 839-8640
WWW.AUTHORHOUSE.COM

First published by AuthorHouse 2/16/2006

ISBN: 1-4208-9338-6 (SC)

Library of Congress Control Number: 2005909453

Printed in the United States of America
Bloomington, Indiana

This book is printed on acid-free paper.

To RMF

ACKNOWLEDGMENTS

Many people contributed to this book in one way or another. I would first like to thank Jill Mateo for her comments on the manuscript, as well as for her encouragement and friendship over many years. Helpful comments were also sent my way by Anna Bess Sorin, Susan Wieland, Cary Anne Cadman, Rose Franco, Barry Yeoman, Heather Heying, Mark Sullivan, Gerald Sorin, Joseph Manson, Susan Perry, Anna-Maria Marshall, Leslie Abbatiello and Rachel Sexton. Any errors and infelicities that remain in the following are entirely my responsibility.

CONTENTS

CHAPTER ONE.   LESBIANS AND GAY MEN IN THE
TWENTIETH CENTURY   I

Evolutionary theory suggests that individual organisms should try to "maximize their reproduction." So for biologists who study social behavior, homosexuality is a puzzle.

CHAPTER TWO.   DARWINIAN FUNDAMENTALISM   15

Why Charles Darwin still matters. An introduction to evolution and the theories of natural selection and sexual selection.

CHAPTER THREE.   REHABILITATING SOCIOBIOLOGY   37

More evolutionary theory and a kinder, gentler sociobiology that suggests that modern human behavior is influenced by the evolutionary history of our species, but certainly is not determined by our genes.

CHAPTER FOUR.   BISEXUAL MONKEYS   59

What can animal behavior tell us about human behavior? How much homosexual behavior is observed in nonhuman primates? How often is that behavior exclusive? Why is exclusivity important?

CHAPTER FIVE.   HEREDITARY HOMOSEXUALITY   79

Since the early 1990s, a number of studies have shown that there may be genetic and anatomical differences between straight people and gay people. Is there a political agenda at the root of studies that suggest that gay people are born that way?

Chapter Six. Queer Neighbors   97

Homosexuality as it has recently been expressed in Western countries does not seem to have been a part of many of the world's traditional cultures. The social construction of sexuality.

Chapter Seven. Three Lives   115

Three cultural traditions that resonate with, but are very different from, recent Western homosexuality: bisexuality among men in ancient Greece, ritualized homosexuality in Melanesia, and the Native American berdache tradition.

Chapter Eight. False Dichotomies   133

If there is a gay gene, how has it been maintained in the human species? The inextricable link between nature and nurture in the evolution of homosexuality.

Chapter Nine. *Homo sapiens* in the Twenty-First Century   159

Politics, sociobiology and the future of a gene for homosexuality.

Endnotes   169

Index   189

PREFACE

This is a book about context.

When I started reading about evolutionary biology, I didn't want to think that what I was reading had any personal relevance for me, for the way I live, or for the lives of people around me. Initially I resisted the ideas that I've written about in this book. Eventually I came around – I haven't become some kind of wild-eyed genetic determinist, but I have come to believe that it is a mistake to ignore our evolutionary history and pretend that it is irrelevant to human behavior.

The basic idea of the evolutionary biology of behavior, to oversimplify, is that individuals (people, crickets, lions, geraniums) have been designed over the course of vast evolutionary time to "maximize their reproduction" – to leave a genetic legacy in the form of offspring. In the past forty years or so evolutionary biology has been invigorated by this approach to behavior. The extent to which this idea is applicable to human behavior, however, remains a controversial topic. It is quite obvious that people are engaged in a whole lot of things that have very little to do with making babies.

There is at least one human characteristic that seems to be completely incompatible with the basic idea of evolutionary biology: some humans only want to have sex with others of the same sex. An exclusive homosexual orientation seems like a very poor way to "maximize" the number of offspring you leave behind. The mere existence of gay people seems to contradict one of evolutionary biology's basic tenets. At the very least, homosexuality seems to suggest that the human species does not follow the same evolutionary rules that other species do.

Some recent studies have suggested that lesbians and gay men are biologically different from heterosexual people. If there is a gene for homosexuality, how exactly might that gene have been maintained in the human species? It seems as if a gay gene would not last for very long if the people who have it are only interested in sex with other people of the same sex. As a *New Yorker* magazine cartoon asked a few years ago, "If homosexuality is inherited, shouldn't it have died out by now?"

This book is an attempt to answer that question.

Some of the scientists who believe that evolutionary biology is relevant to modern humans use this approach to behavior to explain just about everything people do. But human behavior is a lot more complicated than the acting out of urges to pass along genes. If there is a biological basis for homosexuality, it necessarily interacts with human cultures. *Any* biological predisposition for complex human behavior necessarily interacts with the cultures in which people find themselves. The things that people do are the product of the interaction of nature *and* nurture, biology *and* culture, genes *and* environment.

Getting beyond the dichotomous way of thinking that prescribes that human behavior is the result of either nature or nurture (biology or culture, genes or environment) is a difficult task. But the basic concepts of evolutionary biology can point us in the right direction. It is the context that makes sense of much of what we do with our lives. Evolutionary biology does not explain everything, but it does provide a paradigm that supports the idea that human nature exists. Biology and culture work together to make us what we are, whether we are entirely gay, entirely straight, or something in between.

CHAPTER ONE

Lesbians and Gay Men
in the Twentieth Century

It was an extraordinary century for America's lesbians and gay men. In the course of one hundred years, homosexuality evolved from a secret perversion to a very public presence in American culture. In 1900, gay people were mental defectives or sinners. By 2000, lesbians and gay men were out and proud and very visible in the American mass media. Openly gay people were coming soon to a theater near you.

One of the most significant manifestations of gay pride in America occurs annually toward the end of June in the aptly named lesbian and gay pride parades held in many locales around the country. I have been going to New York City's parade for decades. The Pride parade is an event that is something of a cross between a political demonstration and a party for 100,000. It occurs at the end of a full week of rallies, dances and general sign wearing. The last week in June is an unofficial holiday for tens of thousands of lesbians and gay men in and around New York City, and the tens of thousands of people who come to New York from all over the world to participate in the festivities.

In the 1970s, the parade originated in Greenwich Village, long home to many of the City's lesbians and gay men, and marched out of the Village, up Fifth Avenue. Symbolically, as one of my more radical friends explained to me, we were marching "out of the ghetto." (This was said without a trace of irony despite the fact that Greenwich Village includes some of the world's most expensive real estate.) More recently however, the parade has taken off from midtown Manhattan and marched into the Village. In this incarnation, the parade is more like a homecoming. Many people march in the parade, but many others just watch and cheer. By the time the parade reaches the narrow streets of the Village, the crowd is densely packed together, cheering on the Dykes on Bikes who always lead the way, the politicians who trail after them, and the hundreds of groups, bands and floats – and the tens of thousands of people – that make up the rest of the parade.

The groups represented at the parade run the gamut from ministers to self-styled sexual outlaws. The professional groups are all there – the police officers, doctors, lawyers, teachers. There are floats with thumping dance music, political groups calling for gay liberation, and people from twelve-step programs. There are sports leagues, and drag queens in full regalia. There is even, occasionally, a small group behind a sign that reads "Lesbians for Patsy Cline."

Simply everyone is there.

There is, of course, a serious side to the party. While the atmosphere at the parade is akin to that of Mardi Gras, the *fact* of the parade, the simple presence of all those tens of thousands of people, is a statement. Gay people have come out of the closet. The slogan is "We're here, we're queer, get used to it," as in, we are not going to go away. We are not going to beg for the civil rights that heterosexual Americans take for granted.

The New York City Pride parade and others like it throughout the United States commemorate the start of the modern lesbian and gay civil rights movement, which is usually dated to the 1969 Stonewall riots in Greenwich Village. The Stonewall was a bar on Christopher Street near Sheridan Square that had a large drag queen clientele. As a matter of course, the police would raid the Stonewall and other bars like it and arrest the patrons. One night in June 1969, so legend goes, the patrons of the bar had had enough of the police harassment. When the cops tried to close down the club and arrest them, the bar patrons fought back. That event sparked a series of demonstrations over the next few nights in the Village.

Gay people were getting organized, and the cops were about to back down.

Newspaper headlines tell the story in a few words. The first indication that something was brewing was when the *New York Post* ran an article called "Village Raid Stirs Melee" on June 28, 1969. The next day, the *New York Times*, America's paper of record, reported "Four Policemen Hurt in Village Raid." The *Times* ran another story on June 30th headed "Police Again Rout Village Youths," and on July 3rd there was yet another *Times* article beginning with the vague headline "Hostile Crowd Dispersed Near Sheridan Square." If you were not reading beyond the headlines, you would have to have been looking at the more liberal *Village Voice* to find out what these events were really about. On July 3rd, the *Voice* ran a piece called "Gay Power Comes to Sheridan Square."

Why did the gay liberation movement explode out of Greenwich Village that week? Perhaps it was just a coincidence, but the riots began just a few days after the death of gay icon Judy Garland. It was an emotional week for many gay people, in more ways than one.

More generally of course, the late 1960s were a time of great social upheaval in the United States, with movements against the war in Vietnam, for women's rights, and for African American equality. The gay liberation movement, while it may have seemed to emerge fully formed (and fully armed) like Athena from the head of Zeus, actually grew out of a long history of pioneering gay and lesbian organizations that were in existence in the 1950s and 1960s.[1] While gay people may have been nearly invisible to mainstream American culture, early gay rights groups like the Mattachine Society and the Daughters of Bilitis had been working since the early 1950s to project "however faintly, a point of view about same-gender relationships that departed from the consensus of sin, sickness, and criminality."[2] While America had had lesbian and gay citizens for a long time, gay subcultures were not particularly

3

visible to the straight world. This was understandable given that being gay was an official mental illness in the psychiatric industry's Diagnostic and Statistical Manual.[3]

At the time of the Stonewall riots, there were networks of gay men and lesbians in the United States who knew each other through the early so-called homophile organizations, as well as through personal contacts. The general public may not have known about the existence of America's gay subculture, but it was there nonetheless. The change after Stonewall was not that lesbians and gay men abruptly came into existence in American society; it was that they were suddenly much more visible.

The visibility that grew out of the lesbian and gay civil rights movement in the 1970s was only a prelude to the profound change in American culture that took place in the 1980s and 1990s. As the AIDS crisis grew throughout the 1980s, gay people were becoming more and more the focal point of American media. The illness and death of actor Rock Hudson in 1985 was a turning point: an epidemic that had been killing thousands of gay men was brought into the living rooms of middle America via the television news. While portions of the American populace responded with extreme homophobia (and continue to do so), many other Americans got an education. Gay men and lesbians live next door. They hold jobs. They raise families. They pay taxes. Whatever the perspective, at the very least it was no longer possible to deny that gay people exist.

This cultural shift continued in the 1990s, and accelerated as the decade progressed. Lesbians and gay men seemed almost ubiquitous in the American mass media. As many lesbians and gay men were coming out to their families and colleagues, a number of relatively high profile celebrities also made public that they were gay, including singers Elton John, Melissa Etheridge and k.d. lang, as well as actors Ian McKellan and Rupert Everett, and tennis legend Martina Navratilova, among others. In addition to real life stories, gay characters started popping up with great regularity in American films and television shows. While some of these depictions fell back on old stereotypes, a large number of them were positive or neutral. And, much to the dismay of America's political right wing, even neutral is visible.

The high point of gay visibility in the American mass media probably occurred on April 30, 1997. On that night, the lead character of the TV series *Ellen* declared her attraction to a character played by Laura Dern. A couple of weeks before that, the eponymous real-life Ellen DeGeneres had herself announced that she is a lesbian in a *Time* magazine cover story.[4]

Ironically, even as the American media seemed to be confirming the gay liberation slogan "We are everywhere," surveys were suggesting that lesbians and gay men actually make up a much smaller percentage of the American population than had been thought. The widespread idea that gay people make up approximately 10 percent of the population was based on the original report of Alfred Kinsey's Institute for Sex Research at Indiana University, published in 1948.[5] The reports on Kinsey's research were a shock for the American public: with the apparent detachment of a biologist (which he was), Kinsey and his colleagues wrote a taxonomy of American sexual practices, which included a lengthy cataloguing of homosexual behavior.

The Kinsey data indicated that a substantial percentage of American men had at least some homosexual experience at some point in their lives. The often referred to 10 percent figure was actually the number of men who are "more or less exclusively homosexual … for at least three years between the ages of 16 and 55."[6] The number of men in the Kinsey report who were exclusively homosexual throughout their lives after adolescence was 4 percent.[7] This latter figure was not one that was usually quoted, but it is closer to the percentage of gay men in the population that more recent studies have cited. Actually some recent research has indicated that gay people make up an even smaller percentage of the population: in 1994, *Discover* magazine reported that in a survey of more than 3,000 men, approximately 1 percent of the respondents had had only male sexual partners within the past ten years; this was similar to recent French and English studies that placed the number at 1.4 percent.[8] Dean Hamer's widely publicized study of the gay gene (more on this in Chapter Five) used a base rate of 2 percent as the prevalence of male homosexuality in America.[9] And it is widely believed that lesbians comprise a smaller percentage of the population than gay men.

Sexuality however is a difficult subject to research. A 1995 study on the topic of homosexual behavior that also asked its participants about whether or not they had been *attracted* to individuals of the same sex, found that even though it is often not acted upon, a fairly large number of people do report finding themselves attracted to others of the same sex. Somewhere between 16 and 20 percent of both male and female respondents in this study in the United States, United Kingdom, and France reported either homosexual behavior or homosexual attraction since age 15.[10] Attraction is not the same as behavior. Identity is something else yet again: in a homophobic society, people who conduct surveys on sexuality are likely to get more "straight" answers than they should.

It seems that all studies that look at the question of how many people are gay are likely to be problematic in one way or another. For example, surveys are supposed to look at a representative sample of the population they are interested in. If a survey were to exclude residents of San Francisco's Castro district, a magnet for gay men, because it is not representative of the United States as a whole, the survey would miss a sizeable group of people. Gay people have moved to San Francisco in large numbers precisely because it is not representative of the United States as a whole. If, by contrast, a survey on sexuality were done in which only people in San Francisco's Castro were queried, heterosexuals might qualify for inclusion on the endangered species list.

Surveys on sexuality are fraught with problems. Any conclusions that are drawn are very sensitive to how homosexuality is defined and how people are chosen for inclusion in such studies. All that can be said with some certainty is that the number of gay people in America is likely to be larger than surveys suggest. It seems unlikely to be smaller: people sometimes have good reasons not to say they are gay; it is difficult to think of reasons why someone would claim to be gay when they are not. The question of how many lesbians and gay men live in the United States ultimately is an academic one, meaning that it is likely to remain speculative. It will stay that way even though Americans are among the most measured and surveyed populations in the history of humankind. And while there has been a great deal of important research done by Western historians and anthropologists on homosexuality, estimates of how many people were gay in other times and places are even less likely to be a close measure of reality.

Does the question of how many people are lesbian or gay matter anyway? In most ways, it does not. Whether gay people make up 2 percent of the population or 10 percent should have no bearing on civil rights issues. Even at a relatively conservative 2 percent, there are still millions of lesbians and gay men in the United States. My main point here is that regardless of the exact numbers, there is undeniably a small percentage of Americans who are lesbian or gay. I am interested in this fact for a very specific reason: if we consider the American population to be a microcosm of the human *species*, then homosexuality is a trait found in a small but significant portion of the population. This raises an interesting question. Is a homosexual orientation something that has evolved as a human characteristic? I believe that the answer to this question is yes.

All humans are members of the same biological species: *Homo sapiens*. Despite the many visible differences between people, we all have a great deal in common, including millions of years of shared evolution and a heritage as primates (the taxonomic group that includes apes, monkeys and some miscellaneous relatives). The human species, like other species, has been subject to the pressures of evolution by natural selection. Every individual alive today shares this common legacy.

How does this relate to homosexuality? Evolutionary theory predicts that individuals will behave in ways that maximize the number of offspring they contribute to the next generation. Gay people are unlikely to "maximize" offspring, and in fact might well have no biological children at all if they follow their inclinations and have sex only with others of the same sex. And yet, homosexuality exists in the human species. Why? If there is a gene for homosexuality, how is it perpetuated? Logically it seems that a gay gene would never make its way to the next generation and would rather rapidly become extinct if the individuals who have it never have sex with individuals of the opposite sex. Wouldn't a gene for homosexuality ensure its own demise?

Homosexuality is a difficult topic for scientists who study behavior. Apart from the fact that homosexuality seems to contradict one of the basic tenets of evolutionary biology, the topic itself is a political minefield. Purely from an evolutionary perspective, exclusive homosexuality *should not exist*. This is not a moral judgment, it is more of a practical matter. Genes survive because they are reproduced by heterosexual sex. Unfortunately for scientists – many of whom are good liberals – saying that homosexuality "shouldn't" exist makes them sound like right-wing fundamentalists who also think that gay people should not exist, albeit for different reasons. So even though this is a fascinating topic, many evolutionary scientists have stayed away from it, possibly out of reluctance to say things that make them sound homophobic.

One scientist however, Harvard biologist E.O. Wilson, boldly stepped into the political minefield in 1975 when he published his influential book *Sociobiology: The New Synthesis*.[11] He did not escape unscathed. Wilson suggested that homosexuality could evolve in some individuals because of what biologists refer to as kin selection. This concept will be discussed further in subsequent chapters. For now, the gist of this idea is that family members share many of the same genes, so an individual who seems to sacrifice her own reproduction by helping her kin raise their offspring is, in effect, helping to perpetuate her own genes. If a maiden aunt is helping raise her siblings' children, those nieces and nephews are carrying many of the maiden aunt's genes. By helping them out, she is actually helping her own genes prosper.

From the perspective of the survival of particular genes, this is not terribly far-fetched; there is evidence of kin selection in many species. From a political perspective however, Wilson blundered very badly with this suggestion. In 1975, the gay liberation movement was essentially in its infancy. Homosexuality was not nearly as familiar to many people as it is now, and it was not nearly as accepted among the general population. While there were plenty of gay people who had close, strong relationships with their families, there were countless others who were estranged from their biological families. To suggest in 1975 that homosexuality might have evolved because maiden aunts and bachelor uncles were helping their biological families was rather insensitive. At that point in time, many families would not even allow lesbian aunts and gay uncles near the kids, just in case homosexuality was contagious. If Wilson had acknowledged this in his book, and suggested that such homophobia might be something that was the result of a new environment our species finds itself in, he might not have been as widely criticized. Even though he probably had good intentions, Wilson did not even mention that in twentieth century America many lesbians and gay men were estranged from the very families that they theoretically should have been assisting, if kin selection was at the root of the evolution of homosexuality.

When Wilson's *Sociobiology* was published, he was near the leading edge of a larger intellectual movement that suggests that a biological perspective on human behavior is valuable. As someone who was instrumental in the return of this perspective to American culture, Wilson was subject to a lot of criticism. Many people saw in his work a disturbing resurgence of biological determinism. Besides being the title of a weighty science book, "sociobiology" became something of a dirty word in American culture. Although the ideas that Wilson wrote about in his book have become very popular in academia and even among the general public in recent years, the word sociobiology is used much less frequently today than it should be. Even professionals who work in this field more often refer to themselves as evolutionary psychologists, or behavioral ecologists, or say they study behavioral biology or evolutionary anthropology. While there are differences between these academic specialties that are important to their practitioners, all of these fields have in common a belief that evolution has influenced and continues to influence behavior. Sociobiology still sounds like something of a questionable endeavor, but it is a word worthy of rehabilitation.

Sociobiology is not inherently deterministic but it does suggest that biology influences behavior. The difference between biology determining behavior and biology influencing behavior is perhaps a bit subtle but it is essential to keep in mind. If the book *Sociobiology* was indeed a sign that biological determinism was making a comeback in American intellectual life it would have been understandable that many people were leery of Wilson's ideas. Biological determinism has a sordid history, to say the least. Biological differences between people have been used to supposedly justify a variety of oppressive and murderous campaigns in which people have done extraordinary violence to their fellow humans. Perhaps the most egregious example of this in the twentieth century was the Holocaust, in which European Jews were exterminated by the millions because they were "inferior" to the Nazis who were in power. The supposed superiority of the Aryan bloodline was used as a justification for genocide.

Similarly, throughout much of the history of the United States, supposed biological differences between Caucasians and African Americans have been invoked to justify racism. African slaves were barely considered to be human by their white owners and by the American government. Even in the slightly more enlightened twentieth century, some people have held that African-Americans are "inferior" to whites. The thinking, such as it is, is that the genes that white people have somehow make them more intelligent (more human, more valuable) than blacks. This idea is not just wrong, it is reprehensible. When Richard Herrnstein and Charles Murray published *The Bell Curve: Intelligence and Class Structure in American Life*[12] in 1994, their bad science seemed to give a patina of scholarly respectability to the "fact" that African Americans tend to score lower on IQ tests than whites. And, Herrnstein and Murray implied, little could be done to change that. *The Bell Curve* hurt people by perpetuating baseless, racist stereotypes. According to Stephen Jay Gould, it was "a manifesto of conservative ideology," rather than "an academic treatise in social theory and population genetics."[13]

These are two examples of some of the damage caused by people who believe that biology is destiny. There are, of course, many other examples, as so many women (all members of the "inferior" sex) can attest. Is it any wonder that many people shy away from looking at the impact that biology has on human behavior? Wouldn't it be better just to believe that humans are a blank slate at birth and that cultures, which are presumably more malleable than genes, shape the people we become?

It might be more comforting to believe that we have escaped our evolutionary history, but human behavior results from the complex interaction of both our physical bodies and the cultures we inhabit. It is the result of both nature and nurture. In many ways modern people continue to act out the behavioral patterns that have made our lineage successful for the past few million years. We might wish that biology would go away – that people would be somehow better than we are – but we are stuck with bodies and minds that are quite similar to those of our ancestors. Despite all the culture, despite all the technology, despite all the history and philosophy, in many ways people are just relatively hairless primates who walk upright and have a penchant for using tools and language. In at least some features, we are not all that different from chimpanzees and gorillas.

We cannot escape our evolutionary legacy. But there is some good news: there is nothing inherent in the sociobiological paradigm that can be used in any way to justify hate and genocide. If anything, the ideas of modern evolutionary biology, in conjunction with what is known about the history of the human species, provide a powerful rejoinder to those who would use biology to support hatred. People are all members of the same species, *Homo sapiens*. On a profound level, we all have a great deal in common. The history of our species is such that the visible differences between us – the racial and ethnic differences – have evolved only very recently. Strictly from a biological perspective, these differences are essentially meaningless. Despite our divergent cultures, we are all, each and every one of us, entirely human.

While it is quite obvious that there are outward, physical differences among the world's people, the concept of race has been criticized extensively within the scientific community for many years. Grouping people together into different races is an arbitrary endeavor and serves little or no scientific purpose. Even beyond that, "the average difference *between* groups of people living in different parts of the world is much smaller than the differences *among* individuals within each group" (emphasis added).[14] While there is an unfortunate tendency for people to make a very big deal about racial differences, biologically speaking, these differences are often quite literally only skin deep. Up until perhaps 100,000 years ago, Earth's entire human population was small and homogeneous. While 100,000 years sounds like a long time, it is not when you consider the millions of years of shared ancestry from which every person alive today is descended. Something like 100,000 years is an eye blink to evolutionary biologists. Everywhere you find them, people are people.

Sociobiology has had less to say on the topic of homosexuality in humans than you might think, but nevertheless it is a powerful paradigm for understanding human behavior. In order to understand how homosexuality might have evolved, it is necessary to consider what sociobiology says about human behavior more generally. That topic, and the theoretical basis behind it, is what we turn to in the next two chapters.

CHAPTER TWO

Darwinian Fundamentalism

He sat back in his chair, with his arms crossed over his chest, and went silent. After a while, I said, "But humanity is part of nature, too." "Exactly," the pygmy said. "That is exactly the problem."

PHILIP GOUREVITCH, WE WISH TO INFORM YOU THAT TOMORROW WE WILL BE KILLED WITH OUR FAMILIES: STORIES FROM RWANDA[1]

Many educated, liberal Americans have an inconsistent relationship with the concept of evolution. They believe that evolution is a fact: the Earth is billions of years old and various forms of life have appeared and disappeared over time. Fossils are irrefutable evidence that different types of living things have changed over the eons that they have been around. We, as human beings, are decidedly a part of this scenario – our species evolved from some chimpanzee-like creature that existed a few million years ago. You can take a closer look at the fossils of "early man," as well as those of the dinosaurs, at any natural history museum. Depending on your viewpoint, God may or may not have had a hand in evolution, but as any good liberal will tell you, attempts to bring God into the teaching of the origins and diversity of living things is a blatant end run around the separation of church and state. "Creation science" and "intelligent design" are not science; they are religious explanations for the origins of life, and, as such, have no place in public schools.

The typical educated, liberal American viewpoint on evolution becomes inconsistent, however, when you consider the human species more specifically. While liberals usually believe that human *bodies* are the result of millions of years of evolution, human *minds* are often thought to be a *tabula rasa*

15

at birth. What people think, how they feel, the things they believe are thought to be shaped almost entirely by the culture and historical time into which an individual is born. The human brain at birth is a blank slate onto which the world's cultures inscribe our emotions, our desires, and our beliefs. A unitary human nature does not exist because the world's cultures are bewilderingly diverse and people are infinitely malleable.

Sociobiologists have a different view of the human species – one that is much more consistent. From this perspective, both human bodies *and* minds reflect the evolutionary history of the human species. In some ways, people are quite diverse, but their minds are hardly a blank slate at birth. The human brain, just as much as the human body, has been subject to millions of years of evolution by natural selection. And it shows: far from being inexplicably diverse, humans actually have quite a lot in common. That commonality goes by the name of human nature, and the basis for human nature is the fact that we are all members of one species, and we all have minds that were shaped by our shared past.

It is, of course, a matter of perspective whether you choose to emphasize human differences or human commonalities. Much of American social science, in particular cultural anthropology, emphasizes diversity, the differences among the world's people. The thinking here is that because people are raised in different cultures, they have widely divergent ways of viewing the world and varying opinions on right and wrong, good and bad, etc. These differences, so the thinking goes, should be understood in the context of the cultures that produced them. Furthermore, as a general rule, these differences should be celebrated.

Cultural anthropologists often seem appalled by the notion that their area of specialization might be influenced in any way by something as mundane as biology. Sociobiology is a dirty word to many American academics, and the topic is anathema to some educated liberals. To these people it seems like just a short step from recognizing that biology shapes how people live to genetic determinism and genocide. But while sociobiology does not have a particularly optimistic view of the human species, there is nothing inherent in the sociobiological paradigm that is deterministic. What sociobiology suggests is that in order to truly understand human behavior, it is important to understand how humans have evolved as a species. Sociobiologists believe that the human mind is hardly a *tabula rasa*, and this sets people in this field on a collision course with many of their colleagues in academia.

It seems self-evident that the human brain is a vital organ. It is, in fact, something that is quite noticeable about us when people are compared to other animals. Human brains are *big*. They might not be the biggest overall (larger mammals like elephants and whales have larger brains), but they are huge for creatures of our body size. And our brains are very useful. People have abilities that other animals would envy, if they had the capacity for envy. (Incidentally, other animals might find this idea to be amusing, if they had the capacity for humor.) Our brains are quite obviously part of our bodies, and there is no reason to expect that somehow the human brain was exempt from the evolutionary pressures that were exerted on the rest of the organism. So, for example, the human brain is organized in a way that allows an individual to easily learn a language or languages as a young person. Languages include a substantial vocabulary and extremely complex rules of grammar. And yet they are acquired by little children who are otherwise incapable of advanced physical feats. While the specific language an individual learns will depend on what is said in his or her immediate environment, the young human brain is prepared to absorb and then use language.

The basis for sociobiology is the theory of evolution by natural selection. For people who understand how natural selection operates, it seems obvious that an organ like the human brain that is so essential to life must have been subject to strong evolutionary pressures. Views to the contrary naively attempt to place humans above the natural world. But people are not "above" nature, we are decidedly a part of it.

I suspect that many liberals who find the ideas of sociobiology to be repugnant actually just do not understand how evolution works. American science education is not particularly good. Even in a very "blue" state like New York, evolution is just one unit in the high school biology curriculum, rather than the unifying concept around which biology courses could be and should be constructed. And, of course, biology is often optional in college. It can be avoided if someone has a mind to do so. Many people do seem to want to avoid science, and the result is a profound ignorance of biology in our culture. This is one reason that sociobiology seems so threatening to people. Sociobiology is not scary though, and its insights into the human condition can be profound in their own way. The theoretical basis for sociobiology starts with Charles Darwin, the originator of two major evolutionary theories: natural selection and sexual selection.

Darwin was a diffident revolutionary. He was born into a wealthy English family in 1809 (coincidentally on exactly the same day as Abraham Lincoln). As families often do, the Darwins had plans for young Charles. But as a young man, Darwin was frankly a bit of a disappointment to his parents. Instead of pursuing a respectable career in medicine or the clergy, Darwin had an interest of his own, an interest bordering on obsession: he was fascinated by natural history, the study of the natural world.

Natural history has a very Victorian ring to it. It is, in fact, a field that is only rarely studied now. "Doing" natural history involves collecting, organizing and cataloging examples of different kinds of plants and animals. Natural history museums are almost all that remain of this once thriving field of inquiry. Darwin was a collector, but he went well beyond accumulating for the sake of accumulating. He was interested in the *patterns* he saw in the natural world. He was interested in the big picture. By considering the significance of what he observed, Darwin arrived at one of the great theories of science: evolution by natural selection. More will be said about natural selection as this chapter progresses, but for now the concept, in brief, is that species change over time because some individuals have traits which help them to reproduce more than other individuals. As time passes, species change or evolve because of this differential reproduction.

From 1831 to 1836, Darwin sailed around the world as the resident naturalist aboard an English ship, the H.M.S. *Beagle*.[2] The purpose of that particular voyage was a survey of South America. Darwin got the post because the captain of the ship was looking for an educated companion with whom he could discuss intellectual issues. Charles was perfect for the job. Although they were reluctant, the elder Darwins allowed 22-year old Charles to embark. The trip would change him into an established member of the English scientific community; it also changed the history of science.

Darwin was away from England for nearly five years and literally traveled around the world. Most famously, the trip brought him to the Galapagos Islands, in the Pacific Ocean off the coast of Ecuador. This stop was significant because it was there that Darwin saw the finches that he and subsequent biologists were to write so much about.[3] The Galapagos Islands are the home to a number of finch species that are quite similar. Each species is distinct from the others, however, because of one or more traits. The beaks of the different species, for example, are specialized to extract food from different sources and are shaped differently, depending on whether the bird in question eats insects or flowers or seeds or fruits.

This array of similar yet distinct species does not seem to support the idea of a single creation as described in the Bible. (Would God really have made so many kinds of finches?) The

Biblical version was, of course, the prevailing explanation in Europe for the origin of life at the time of Darwin's voyage. The Galapagos finches are obviously closely related, but they are specialized for different ways of making a living. Did God create each of these types of birds individually, or did these birds descend from a common ancestor? The latter seemed more likely to Darwin.

In addition to the extraordinary variety of animals and plants Darwin saw on his around-the-world cruise, he also saw many fossils. Most significantly, Darwin was seeing fossils unlike those of his native Europe. Often, the fossils resembled the animals that still lived in the place in question. This suggested to Darwin that particular types of animals had changed over time and were the ancestors, in specific locales, of the fauna still found in those places today. Perhaps the Biblical account of creation didn't tell the whole story. Perhaps Europe was not the entire universe.

Darwin saw and collected vast amounts of information indicating that living things had evolved over long periods of time. The Biblical account of creation suggested that species were created once – a few thousand years ago according to the standard thinking of the time. Species would have had little time to change since God was done making them in 4,004 B.C.[4] Unlike many of his contemporaries, however, Darwin believed that the Earth was considerably older than the Bible indicated. Fossils and arrays of similar species like the finches on the Galapagos Islands were strong evidence that the story of life on Earth was more complicated than a literal reading of the Bible would suggest.

The concept of evolution as such did not originate with Charles Darwin – the idea that living things had changed over time had been growing in popularity among European scientists in the nineteenth century. Jean Baptiste de Lamarck, for example, had suggested that evolution happened because characteristics that were acquired during an organism's lifetime were inherited by its offspring. With natural selection, Darwin came up with what has come to be recognized as *the* explanation for how evolution actually functions. Evolution is a fact; Darwin's theory of natural selection explained the mechanisms behind that fact. That evolution had occurred was already fairly well known to a small group of Victorian scientists; how it worked was Darwin's contribution.

In retrospect, natural selection was a brilliant idea, but Darwin was reluctant to publish. Why? Again, Darwin was kind of shy for a revolutionary. He was also well aware that his ideas would not make him popular with the religious standard-bearers in England. He was a cautious man who was afraid to rock the boat. Many years passed after the voyage of the *Beagle* before Darwin went public with his ideas. Eventually, Darwin was forced to publish because someone else had come up with exactly the same theory. Alfred Russel Wallace, another English naturalist, sent Darwin a paper in which he outlined the very ideas that Darwin had been developing and nursing for so long. In 1858, Darwin and Wallace jointly presented a paper to a scientific society in London describing the theory of evolution by natural selection. The following year, Darwin's *The Origin of Species by Means of Natural Selection* was published.[5]

The Origin starts with a chapter on domesticated species. It was well known to Darwin and to others that domesticated animals and plants could be selectively bred by farmers to produce desired characteristics. So, for example, if two sheep with particularly fine wool are mated, they are likely to produce offspring with particularly fine wool. An individual cow that gives a lot of milk could be bred in preference to a less productive cow and there was a good chance her female offspring would likewise give more milk. While the differences between the sheep or the cows in a particular herd might be small, incremental changes over generations could be exploited over time to produce desired characteristics.

People had a hand in creating the various breeds of dogs and other animals that they had domesticated. Human choice had given the Victorian world many different kinds of dogs, as well as cows that produced a lot of milk and sheep that produced fine wool. People had selected the characteristics they wanted to emphasize in the animals they kept, and then by breeding animals selectively, they were able to change the species. This *artificial selection* – as opposed to allowing domesticated animals to breed at random – was a human production.

Darwin's genius was that he extrapolated this idea to the natural world. The variation seen in domesticated animals (in milk production, in quality of wool, etc.) parallels that seen in nature. Also, just as in domesticated animals, at least some of the variation among members of a particular species is inherited from parent to offspring. Sheep with fine wool will likely produce more sheep with fine wool. Why? Darwin did not know about genes; DNA would not be deciphered for another century. Nonetheless Darwin saw evidence everywhere that differences between individuals of one generation are often expressed in the same or similar ways in their respective offspring. (Although his work was unknown to Darwin, a monk named Gregor Mendel was doing research in the latter half of the nineteenth century that would form the basis for the field of genetics. Darwin's and Mendel's ideas were combined in the 1920s and 1930s in the "modern synthesis" of evolutionary biology.[6])

Darwin also knew of the work of economist Thomas Malthus.[7] Malthus saw a universal pattern in the natural world: living things have an extraordinary capacity for reproduction. Being an economist, Malthus was mostly concerned with the impact that this has on humans. He argued that if left unchecked, human populations will increase at a very rapid or geometric rate. Food supplies, by contrast, will increase only at an arithmetic or much slower rate. Demand for food will quickly outstrip the supply, and famine will be the inevitable result. Human populations have the capacity to reproduce in great numbers, but the necessary food supplies are not as easily obtained.

Again, Darwin extrapolated. He understood that all types of living things have an extraordinary capacity for reproduction – all kinds of living things can produce far more offspring than can possibly survive. Some, but by no means all, of the offspring that are produced will reach adulthood and reproduce themselves.

How does all this add up? Living things vary and there are not enough resources to go around. What ensues is what Darwin referred to as a "struggle for existence." Differences between individuals that in any way help them procure the resources they need to survive will result in differential reproduction: some individuals will reproduce more than others because they have traits that help them compete. Organisms with variations favored by the environment at any given time will survive, thrive and reproduce. Those with less favored variations might not survive, they might not thrive, and they might not reproduce. Or they might not reproduce as much.

Individuals with the favored variations are better *adapted* to their environments. They will have more offspring and their offspring will likely inherit the variations that made their parents successful. If the environment stays stable, the cycle perpetuates itself. If the environment changes, a different variant might be better adapted to the new circumstances. This is natural selection: some living things will out-compete others because they have traits that are better suited to their environment. Over long spans of time and many generations, species change because some traits are favored over others.

Finally, with Darwin, the Western world had an explanation for why life is nasty, brutish and short, as Thomas Hobbes had pointed out in the seventeenth century. Nature, as Tennyson said, is red in tooth and claw. Herbert Spencer chimed in and pointed out that it is survival of the fittest. This is not exactly a sunny outlook. Unfortunately that does not make it incorrect.

In a sense, nature is remarkably wasteful. Living things can and do reproduce themselves extravagantly, but only a small subset of their offspring will survive. The rest of the kids are destined for an early demise. Sometimes chance is a factor in survival and reproduction, but, again, Darwin was thinking about the big picture. While some specific individual organisms might reproduce or not based on elements that are little more than capricious, over long spans of time, over millions of years of evolutionary time, species change.

Natural selection is, in some ways, a creation story, similar to the Bible and creation stories found in cultures throughout the world. Darwin's version of the creation story is all about competition. You might argue that this was no accident: like everyone else, Darwin was a product of his times. The theory of natural selection is redolent of capitalism in Victorian England. Actually, redolent is too pleasant a word. Natural selection reeks of Victorian era capitalism.

To illustrate natural selection in action, the following is a Darwinian creation story. Picture this: a prototypical female mammal, perhaps some variety of rodent, is living on her own in a primeval forest. She is not entirely alone in the forest though, and eventually finds herself pregnant. The father of the soon-to-be-born offspring has not stayed around (it is unusual for male mammals to stay around), so when she goes into confinement, she is by herself.

Say she gives birth to a litter of four (multiple offspring are common in mammals). From the kids' perspective, the competition starts at birth (if not before[8]). The mother is nursing them for the first few weeks, but if times are tough, she might not have enough milk for all the kids. Lactation is an energetically costly undertaking for the mother, and her four offspring will compete against each other for the limited milk supply. They are also in competition with their siblings for other things that their mother provides: protection, attention, and assistance.

The prototypical female mammal does, of course, have a strong interest in the survival of her offspring, but she also has to fend for herself. She has to find food for herself to stay alive; she also has to find food so that she can make more milk for her offspring. Furthermore, she shouldn't throw everything she's got into this one litter of offspring – assuming she survives and mates again, she will have future litters. If times are good and food for the female mammal is plentiful, she might make enough milk for all the offspring. More than likely though, not all of the offspring will survive.

It is even possible that no one at all survives from the litter, but for the sake of the story, let's say one kid makes it. It might have been kind of tough going this far, and this is only the beginning. As it grows up, the second generation prototypical mammal has to survive moving away from its mother and finding its own territory; it has to survive the predators that think it looks a lot like a meal; it has to find its own food; it has to survive any injuries and illnesses it might experience.

Even if the second generation mammal manages to out-compete her siblings for everything she needs from mom, and even if she has survived moving out onto her own, she will learn quickly that she is not the only mammal in the primeval forest. There are lots of other animals nearby and they all have kids and everybody is hungry. More than likely, there just is not enough to go around. If the second generation mammal has some trait, some feature that makes her more competitive, maybe she will survive. Maybe she will make it through to a point where she herself can reproduce.

She might have survived so far because she was the quickest of her littermates to nurse from their mother. She might have survived because she was the most cautious of her littermates. She might have survived because she was the smallest of the lot and was able to hide when a predator came along. She might have survived because she was the first to cross the stream to an unoccupied territory. Whatever the reason, if this second generation mammal reproduces, her offspring might be like their mother and that similarity might contribute in turn to their survival.

If the mammalian population in the primeval forest is stable, an average female mammal will probably produce two surviving offspring over the course of her lifetime.[9] The average female might produce more offspring in an expanding population, but she might produce fewer offspring if the population is shrinking. Let's do some math. Most years are, by definition, average. If the prototypical female mammal has two litters of four offspring each year over the course of four average years, she will give birth to 32 offspring over the course of her lifetime. If her success in raising those kids is average, she will see two of the 32 kids survive to adulthood and go on to reproduce themselves. In other words, 30 of 32 or nearly 95% of her offspring will die without reproducing. The prototypical female mammal will be the mother of a lot of dead babies over the course of her lifetime. Infant mortality is huge in nature.

People have an unusual perspective on infant mortality. The human population has been expanding at an astronomical rate for about the last 10,000 years or so, since the beginnings of agriculture. While infant mortality has been and continues to be an important issue among human populations, generally the human species has had a great run of reproductive success since the dawn of history. People in the United States today, for example, have an expectation that the large majority of children that are born will survive to adulthood. A mortality rate of almost 95% before reproductive age is inconceivable.

Another way that humans are atypical mammals is that the males of our species are much more involved with their offspring than is the case in most other species. If the prototypical female mammal had had the prototypical male mammal around to help with the kids and to provide some sustenance, she might not have had that 95% loss rate. But the prototypical male mammal's strategy is to let the female fend for herself, because his best bet in terms of maximizing reproduction is to mate with other females and let each of them do her best to raise the offspring.

In general, living things have the capacity to reproduce themselves abundantly, but living things also vary in the strategies that they use for reproduction.[10] Some species produce wildly extravagant numbers of offspring and only a tiny, tiny fraction of them survive to adulthood. Fish, for example, tend to produce thousands of eggs but over the course of their reproductive lifetimes, only a few if any of the eggs are likely to result in another adult-sized fish that reproduces. Similarly, insects generally produce huge numbers of eggs and very few of the resulting offspring will survive. Other species, by contrast, tend to produce a smaller number of offspring and then care for them more extensively. The prototypical female mammal, for example, in producing a litter of four is actually on the conservative side compared to other types of living things. Mammals, by definition, produce milk that is provided from mothers to offspring and this qualifies them as extensive caregivers when compared to many types of fish or insects that will lay a vast number of eggs and then just move along and let any resulting kids fend for themselves.

The primates are among the champion caregivers. Humans are classified as primates and, like others in this group, give birth to only one or two offspring at a time. Humans, like other primates, then spend an inordinate amount of time and resources on each of these kids, hoping that they will survive and reproduce. Each kid gets more attention, and thus is more likely to survive. But this is a risky strategy in its own way because putting so much into a few kids increases the possibility that random events will wipe out a parent's life's work. It could be the classic mistake of putting all your eggs into one basket. Even at this low rate of reproduction – one or two kids at a time – primates still have the capacity to reproduce themselves many times over, over the course of a lifetime.

Why does all this potential life go unrealized? Why all the dead babies? While it seems like a remarkable waste of effort and waste of resources, this way of doing things has worked out well over the course of evolutionary time for a number of reasons. For one thing, each new offspring is genetically unique and has a shot at being the best of its kind. For another thing, this overproduction of offspring allows opportunities to be exploited. If times are good, many kids might survive. Similarly, many kids might survive if a new territory opens up. Say the prototypical female mammal described earlier had been the only female mammal in the forest. Food for her is plentiful, more of her offspring survive and soon her offspring and their offspring are all over the primeval forest. The prototypical female mammal has hit the genetic jackpot. While the prevailing circumstances in the natural world might seem like a remarkable waste of time, energy, resources and babies, natural selection works and it has worked since the beginning of life on Earth.

What is the prize in the struggle for existence? The prize is reproduction. The prototypical female mammal goes through all those trials and tribulations because she is attempting to achieve a bit of genetic immortality. She is working hard to ensure that some portion of her will continue on into the future. Her offspring are taking her genes with them when they venture out into the world, and she has invested a lot in their success.

All living things are descended from creatures that struggled, survived and reproduced. We are all descended from individuals who did not give up. It is a matter of logic: the creatures that metaphorically said "Why bother?" are not our ancestors. The ones that did not struggle or who lost the fight are no one's ancestors. Their particular configuration of genes died with them.

This view of animal behavior is the prevailing idea in biology at this time. Zoologists look at animal behavior as if reproduction is what the animals "want." This is not conscious on the part of the animals in question, but if you take the desire for reproduction and a shot at genetic immortality as a starting point, nearly all observed animal behavior makes sense. Organisms that do not survive obviously do not reproduce, and those that do not reproduce, while they may survive to a ripe old age, leave no descendants. Their genes are an evolutionary dead end without reproduction.

The concept of natural selection was Charles Darwin's great contribution to biology. Before we move on to discuss how twentieth century biologists have interpreted Darwin's theory, it should be mentioned that Darwin was also responsible for another important idea in evolutionary biology. Again, the theory of natural selection emphasized that organisms engage in a "struggle for existence." But there are some traits that seem to have evolved even though organisms might be better off without them. Indeed, some species have traits that seem to be downright deleterious to their survival. The classic example is the tail of the peacock. A male peacock has a huge, elaborate tail that, when unfurled, is quite beautiful. Beauty comes at a price though: the peacock must lug the tail around all the time, even if it is unfurled and gorgeous only part of the time. The tail is heavy and interferes with the peacock's mobility. So, why bother? A peacock without the elaborate tail would be much more mobile and would probably lead a longer life by going tail-less since it could more easily evade animals that prey on it. The tail of the peacock is an extreme example, but often, in birds especially, males are brightly colored or otherwise very noticeable. Why? Why males in particular? Wouldn't it make more sense to lay low?

Survival and a long life are not the only considerations. Darwin came up with the concept of sexual selection to explain why some characteristics are maintained or elaborated upon in species, even though the features themselves might not seem to be conducive to the survival of individuals.[11] Some traits have developed primarily because they help their bearers to attract the attention of the opposite sex. So, male peacocks have those elaborate tails because they attract the attention of females of the species. A male who does not have a large, cool tail might live a long life himself, but he probably will not reproduce. His genes would not be passed along to the next generation.

There are two basic component parts to Darwin's theory of sexual selection: male-male competition and female mate choice.[12] Females do not always have a choice about with whom they will mate. In a number of primate species, for example, the males are a lot bigger than the females and females can be coerced into sex with a particular male through violent behavior or threats of violence. But quite often females do have choices. Since primatologists cannot read the minds of the monkeys and apes they are studying, the choice a particular female makes is open to a lot of interpretation.

Often people who study animal behavior simply do not know why a female will choose to mate with one male rather than another. There are many theories, but the answer often comes down to the idea that the chosen male has "good genes." This is pretty vague and perhaps a bit circular, but even this "*Je ne sais quois*" theory actually has some rationale behind it. If a male is chosen because he is attractive to the female in question for whatever reason, her sons, if they resemble their father, might also be attractive to females. So while we might not see the appeal of a particular male monkey, if a female monkey does and she mates with him, her sons might also have appeal to female monkeys. The sons, like their father before them, might get to mate more often than the less appealing males. The female choosing the attractive male might well wind up having more grandchildren than a female who mates with any random male.

Sometimes females have no choice about whom they will mate with because only one male is available. This probably is not because there is only one male in the neighborhood, but rather there is only one male available because the males have been competing among themselves for the privilege of mating with the females. Competition between males is the second component part of Darwin's theory of sexual selection. It should not be necessary to go into too much detail about competition between males. Any daily newspaper will provide as many examples as necessary to illustrate this point. The sports section of the *New York Times* is an amusing place to start.

While competitive males sounds like a stereotype (everyone, after all, knows some competitive females as well as some non-competitive males), it is worth keeping in mind that this pattern is extremely widespread in the animal world. There are nice, cooperative daddy types among primates, for example, but males who are battling it out among themselves for opportunities to mate with females are very frequently observed. Think of antlers. Think of tusks. Think of those huge canine teeth on monkeys that look like they would interfere with eating. Even if they do interfere, pity the poor male baboon who doesn't have them – he will be at a disadvantage if there is a female who is ready to mate nearby, as well as another male who does have those big sharp canine teeth. Even in cases where the males of a species don't have an obvious distinguishing feature, they frequently have something with which to fight among themselves and with which to bully the females: greater size. The bigger males fighting over the available female is a reliably observed phenomenon in the animal world.

Darwin's theory of sexual selection predicts that males will be competitive and females will be choosy and coy because they are looking for the "best" fathers for their offspring. This sounds like such a blatant sexist stereotype that it is tempting to dismiss the whole concept. Males are not wanton competition machines, and again, everyone knows some pretty competitive females, as well as the occasional coy male. (Darwin himself was not immune to the temptation to play it coy once in awhile: he knew that *The Origin of Species* would rock the Victorian world, but one of the few statements about the human species in that book was that "Light will be thrown on the origin of man and his history."[13]) Looking at the big picture though, as a *general pattern* among animals, males are somewhat more competitive than females, and females are somewhat more selective about sex than males. This pattern does not hold true all the time, but Darwin's theory of sexual selection suggests why the behavior is seen so often.

Darwin's ideas about sex differences and sexual selection were elaborated upon in the 1970s by American biologist Robert Trivers.[14] Trivers took Darwin's ideas as a starting point and interpreted behavior (in particular sex differences in behavior) in terms that sound like they are right out of an economics text. Trivers's genius was that he thought about behavior in terms of investments. If survival and reproduction are the twin goals of animal life, what is keeping any given individual from achieving those goals? Males and females need some similar things to survive, such as food, shelter and the skills to avoid predators. Beyond that, however, males and females have somewhat different concerns. What limits a female in the achieving the goal of reproduction? Usually the availability of resources – food, shelter, safety, time. Access to a male usually is not much of an issue for females – males who are available for sex are a dime a dozen in most species. A male by contrast needs food, shelter, safety, time *and* he needs access to females. His reproduction is limited by access to females. Willing females are harder to find than willing males.

A female also needs access to a male (for the sperm obviously), but in general, females will invest more resources in her offspring than males will. This is especially true in mammals. In mammals, the females invest a huge amount of time and resources in their offspring. In many animal species, females are very busy doing most of the work of having and raising kids. It takes a long time for a female mammal to successfully send a kid out into the world. The females make a large investment in gestation and lactation, and their time and resources are valuable. Males fight for females because females will kick in most of the work involved in having offspring. Males have to have access to females to achieve genetic immortality; females can do *almost* all of it on their own.

(If the concept of parental investment does not sound applicable to humans in America in the twenty-first century where women seem to compete intensely among themselves for men, keep in mind that humans are somewhat atypical mammals in that men very often make a substantial investment of resources in their children. Sex differences in parental investment are not as great in humans as they are in many other mammals. Also, when you consider that men tend to die younger than women, that more men than women are gay, and that more men than women are in prison, the number of men available for committed relationships is smaller than the number of women available in twenty-first century America. Intense competition among women for men ensues.)

If you accept that a goal of much behavior of nonhuman animals is reproduction, then males and females have fundamentally different interests when it comes to sex. A female mammal has to devote a lot of time and energy to any given offspring in order to successfully send it out into the world. She wants to get the best father she can for her offspring, so coy and choosy works for females. The contribution of a male mammal to his offspring may, by contrast, be no more than the energy that is required to have sex once. A male mammal who wants to reproduce again is only limited by his access to another fertile female. Female mammals are left figuratively and often literally holding the baby. And, significantly, a female mammal frequently does not have much use for males again until the kid she is lugging around is pretty grown up and has stopped nursing. It is only then that the female is interested in mating again.

The theory of parental investment was quite a revelation to me as a feminist. I do not mean to imply by any means that biology *should be* destiny, but the fact is that biology *has been* destiny for many women in many cultures. Female oppression started here, with some very fundamental sex differences. Male animals are limited in reproduction by their access to females, and among humans, sexism and the objectification of women are extremely widespread. This is not a coincidence. Male animals need access to females in order to reproduce; human males in myriad cultures are obsessed with controlling women and their reproductive potential. This is not a coincidence either. Patriarchy arose all over the world from some basic biological differences between males and females.[15]

As with the case of Darwin's competitive males and choosy females, Trivers's ideas sound remarkably sexist on the surface. Males are limited by their access to females ... so males will always be on the lookout for sex. For females, more sex probably will not translate into more offspring, so why bother? Cultures, of course, have a lot to say about sexuality. There are cultural reasons why men might be more enthusiastic about sex than women. For example, a reputation as a bit of a slut for a woman is usually thought to be a bad thing; for a man, a reputation as a bit of a stud might be considered to be a good thing; the same behaviors underlie these reputations. The slut and the stud are stereotypes, but these ideas arose out of something. Are there fundamental differences between men and women? I think there are. This is not to say that sexism is good or that discrimination against women is good, but on the whole, women and men, on average, do have somewhat different interests, and cultures amplify these differences.

Sex differences are not inherently bad. It is bad though when mild differences between men and women harden into stereotypes (or even laws) that limit people's options in life.

It is the rules that people make about sex differences that cause harm. It is the opinions and expectations about those differences and the rigidity with which people approach them that cause problems. There is a great deal of overlap between men and women in terms of attitudes toward sex, love, marriage and children. The bad stuff comes up when cultural rules rigidly prescribe how men and women should behave.

Like the good liberal depicted at the beginning of the chapter, the stereotypical feminist finds sociobiology to be really distasteful. But that is groundless: the ideas of evolutionary biology do not say that women *should be* consigned to secondary lives in the world today. But the fact is that women have been and continue to be oppressed in many or perhaps most cultures. The idea that this might have arisen because of some fundamental sex differences actually can be quite enlightening. Women are oppressed in cultures all over the world. Was this oppression invented anew each time? I think not. Understanding sex differences from an evolutionary perspective can shed a lot of light on a very old problem.

While the feminist party line might be that fundamental sex differences are either nonexistent or irrelevant, people with some knowledge of evolutionary biology believe otherwise. Anyone who has been around young children probably also believes otherwise. Even without cultural elaboration, it is frequently the case that girls will be girls and boys will be boys. Even if the Barbie doll isn't thrust into the little girl's hands, she might want the Barbie doll. Even if the little boy isn't told that he should go out there and play tough with the other little boys, he might just do it anyway. Sometimes these things occur much to the dismay of parents who are well aware of gender stereotypes.

The good news is that even if some degree of biological sex differences will always be with us, the cultural rules that we live by can be re-written. We have seen this to a certain extent in America in the past several generations. The women's movement may not have accomplished anywhere near all its goals, but things are generally better for women now than when I was growing up in the sixties and seventies.

Feminists should take a closer look at evolutionary biology. It is not scary and it has great explanatory value. Knowing where we are starting from is key. A lack of understanding of biology and a lack of interest in sociobiology has actually hampered the women's movement and made it less believable. Generally speaking, people understand that men and women are different from each other in some fundamental ways. The women's movement loses credibility by not embracing that reality.

Robert Trivers's contribution to evolutionary biology was not limited to the concept of parental investment. In the next chapter we will look at another of his influential ideas, as well as the ideas of other twentieth century interpreters of Darwin's ideas about evolution.

CHAPTER THREE

Rehabilitating Sociobiology

She had been brought up in a world which defined a woman as someone who had babies and now she hardly knew what she was or why. Reason told her that there must be more to life than simply passing it on, but emotion told her otherwise.

FAY WELDON, BIG GIRLS DON'T CRY[1]

Robert Trivers's concept of parental investment is one of the foundations of modern behavioral biology. It is called "parental investment" because Trivers suggested that males and females "invest" different amounts of time and energy in their offspring. This is particularly true in species of mammals (including humans), because a child grows within a female's body and then, after it is born, it is nursed by its mother. Both gestation and lactation require a lot of female energy. Males, by contrast, often do not have to invest that much energy while their offspring are growing and are free to pursue other objectives, like mating with other females. Because of this sex difference, males and females have fundamentally different ways of approaching the world.

Robert Trivers was also responsible for another important idea in twentieth century evolutionary biology. This time, instead of sex differences, Trivers attempted to explain why individuals are often seen being nice to each other. Why does this need to be explained?

If it is true that individuals compete among themselves for access to limited resources, as suggested by Darwin's theory of natural selection, you would expect that individuals will always be acting in their own self-interest. But that does not seem to be true: animals are frequently seen being nice to each other. If being nice costs the actor something, that niceness is known as altruism. Altruism is something of a problem in evolutionary biology because, like homosexuality, it "shouldn't" exist. If individuals are supposed to be reproducing at all costs, why are individual primates, for example, so frequently behaving altruistically toward each other?

A simple answer would be that they are being nice to each other because it is for the greater good of the group. Unfortunately, most evolutionary biologists do not think that this works as a strategy. (You could argue that this says a lot about evolutionary biologists.) Natural selection is thought to be acting on *individuals* within groups, rather than on groups as a whole. This is what Darwin thought and biologists since his time have generally also come to that conclusion. So, for example, a male baboon that says "No, after you" to another male baboon is not going to get the girl baboon. His genes are not going to prosper. And the prospects of convincing a whole group of male baboons to act in the collective best interest is well nigh impossible.

Altruism is a problem in evolutionary biology because individuals are the action spot in natural selection. Biologists believe that if there are costs involved, individuals do very little, if anything, "for the good of the group." The idea that they do is somewhat more appealing but unfortunately turns out to be something of a romantic myth. For example, people often mention lemmings when this idea is discussed. Lemmings are small rodents similar to mice that are found in very cold regions of the Northern Hemisphere. They are famous for what looks like mass suicide: thousands of lemmings seemingly throwing themselves into the sea in a self-sacrificial, noble gesture that is supposed to be for the good of the species as a whole.

Actually what is going on is that lemmings experience wild fluctuations in their population size and when the animals become overcrowded, they take off in mass migrations to find some breathing room.[2] What looks like it might be altruistic suicide is in fact mass panic that can result in mass death. Lots of lemmings die at certain times but there isn't anything even remotely noble or self-sacrificial about it.

There is a cartoon by Gary Larson that illustrates the main problem with the idea that individuals are doing things for the good of the group. It is a drawing of a lot of little lemmings rushing into the sea. Unlike his compatriots though, one of the lemmings wears a smile and a life preserver. The basic problem with the "for the good of the group" thinking is that it is possible for an individual to cheat in a group. And it probably is not too hard to cheat (though it could be tricky to find a lemming-size life preserver). Groups made up of individuals that regularly behave in self-negating ways are likely to be swamped in short order by groups in which individuals are consistently acting on their own behalf.

Say there is a group of animals in which all individuals are behaving for the good of the group. If that group is infiltrated by a selfish individual, the selfish individual will probably reproduce more than the others in the group. His genes will thrive at the expense of the altruistic genes of the nicer individuals. Eventually his genes will predominate. If it were possible to detect a selfish individual in an otherwise altruistic group, it might be possible for the altruistic group to continue as such by ostracizing the offending selfish individual. But there is no guarantee that selfish individuals can be detected or stopped.

Darwin focused on the individual as the place where natural selection acts. Over the century and a half since Darwin, biologists have flirted with the idea that certain behaviors are for the good of the group or even for the good of the species. This is more appealing as a concept but unfortunately it just does not seem to be true. In nature, the motto clearly is "look out for number one."

Biologists since Darwin have confirmed that the individual is of primary importance in natural selection. Only a small percentage of observed animal behavior is not selfish. Of that small percentage, the evolution of some niceness is accounted for by another of Robert Trivers's ideas: reciprocal altruism.[3] Individuals sometimes are nice to each other because they have expectation that the favor might be reciprocated or returned at a later date.

Reciprocal altruism is likely to work only if the individuals in question are going to see each other again. If two animals are not going to run into each other again, there is little incentive for altruism. Because of this, you would expect that reciprocal altruism would be more important among animals that live in groups rather than those who live by themselves. Most primates live in groups. Humans are primates who likely evolved in social groups in which there was a good chance of running into the same individuals over and over again. Reciprocal altruism was probably a significant factor in human evolution. It makes sense to be nice under some circumstances, especially if the individual you are being nice to will remember you and will have an opportunity to return the favor later on. Among primates, the cliché "You scratch my back, I'll scratch yours" is frequently, and sometimes literally, true.

Other examples of behaviors that appear to be altruistic can be explained by a concept in evolutionary biology that was suggested by British biologist W.D. Hamilton in the early 1960s. Hamilton broadened the concept of reproduction as an individual's goal with the idea of "inclusive fitness." Inclusive fitness *includes* the reproduction of other individuals who share the same genes. Hamilton was one of the first biologists to view behavioral evolution from the perspective of genes. In order to understand this gene-centered view, it is important to understand how genes are shuffled during the process of sexual reproduction. Genes are little snippets of DNA. DNA (or DeoxyriboNucleic Acid) is a complex molecule that contains the blueprints for living things. All living things have DNA, but the blueprints contain very different instructions for how to build an individual, depending on whether the DNA belongs to a human, a cat or an oak tree. Humans and other species have DNA clustered in packages called chromosomes in each of their cells. Each human cell contains 46 of those packages. In sexual reproduction, some DNA from each parent is combined to make a new human who will also have 46 packages of DNA. Logically, you cannot add together *two full sets* of 46 chromosomes if the end result can only have 46 chromosomes, so some cells undergo a process to reduce the chromosome number by half. This process occurs in the ovaries in females and the testes in males.

Human egg cells produced by the ovaries have 23 chromosomes, and sperm cells produced in the testes also have 23 chromosomes. When egg and sperm cells fuse in sexual reproduction, new individuals are produced that have a full complement of DNA, no more and no less than 46 chromosomes.

The upshot of this, and the reason it is important from an evolutionary perspective, is that family members share DNA. Individuals have exactly half of their mother's DNA and exactly half of their father's because of the DNA contribution made to egg and sperm, respectively. An individual's brothers and sisters also received DNA from the same parents. It is theoretically possible that you do not share any DNA with a full sibling because she inherited their *other* 23 chromosomes from each of your parents. It is also theoretically possible that your full sibling inherited exactly the same chromosomes that you did, but both of these possibilities are statistically negligible. The way the math works out is that *on average*, you are related to a full sister or full brother by about 50%.

For relatives who are more distantly related, it is possible to calculate how much DNA you are likely to share. So, for example, if your brother (with whom you share 50% of your DNA) has a child with someone to whom you are unrelated (someone with whom you share 0% of your DNA), the resulting niece or nephew probably has about 25% of your DNA. The basic rule for figuring out how much DNA is shared between related individuals involves counting the instances of sexual reproduction that separate you. Each time sexual reproduction occurs with an unrelated individual, your DNA is diluted by ½ in the offspring. (But perhaps you don't want to think about that too much since it might require pondering Uncle Fred and Aunt Madge having sex.)

Back to the problem of altruism. W.D. Hamilton considered the degrees of relatedness between family members and suggested that altruism might not be so altruistic after all if you consider that quite often nice behavior is directed toward kin. Since your kin share much of your DNA, if your nice behavior helps them in any way that contributes to their survival and will eventually result in their having more offspring, your niceness is actually in your best interest in the long run because they will be reproducing copies of *your* DNA.

The paradox of altruism (why would an animal incur the cost of being nice with no apparent benefits?) is diminished considerably if the altruism that is observed is primarily directed toward close kin. And that is frequently the case in animal behavior. While the simplest and most direct method of propagating your DNA might be to reproduce, you can also help ensure that copies of your genes make it into the next generation by acting in ways that will aid your relatives in their quest for reproduction.

Hamilton's idea is known as inclusive fitness because it looks at reproduction of DNA that *includes* copies of genes that are found in relatives, as well as those in a particular individual. Hamilton's key publication was a mathematical analysis in which he showed that a hypothetical "gene for altruism" could survive and thrive in nature if it is shared by related individuals.[4]

Inclusive fitness is at the root of the idea of kin selection. In this variant of Darwinian natural selection, *families* are likely to reproduce more or less than other *families* because of the traits that result from their shared DNA. It has been suggested that homosexuality evolved as a sort of extreme kin selection in which individuals forego reproducing themselves in order to devote themselves to furthering their relatives' reproduction. Thus the argument could be made that a gay gene can survive and even spread whether or not the individuals who express the trait of homosexuality actually themselves reproduce. The gay gene might thrive because the nieces and nephews a non-reproductive individual is raising also carry that gene.

Non-reproductive individuals are found in a few species. For example, in many social insects, a class of individuals has evolved that devotes itself to the kin group. These individuals do not reproduce themselves, but because of the way their DNA is set up and passed along, the non-reproductive group is ensuring the survival of their own genes by ensuring the survival of their kin.[5] Because of an unusual genetic system, non-reproductive worker ants, for example, share ¾ of their DNA. An ant that spends her time raising her sisters sees her own genes prosper in future generations, even though she herself never reproduces.

The idea that kin selection might be at the root of homosexuality in humans is not particularly compelling, but this topic will be discussed again later in this book in the context of the evolution of homosexuality. For now, keep in mind that the fact that ants share ¾ of their DNA makes them very different creatures from human siblings who share ½ of their DNA.

Individuals share genes with their parents, their siblings, their offspring and other relatives. The more closely related individuals are, the more DNA they typically share. From an evolutionary perspective, altruism or general benevolence toward others to whom an individual is related is viewed as behavior that is ultimately selfish. By assisting kin, an individual is in effect helping to propagate her or his own genes. While this may seem like a cynical idea, it is one that is borne out by much animal and human behavior. This is not to say that people only do nice things for relatives, but when push comes to shove, inclusive fitness is the basis for the cliché that "blood is thicker than water." This concept has a long history among living creatures.

W.D. Hamilton was one of the first biologists to look at evolution from the gene's perspective. Richard Dawkins, another British biologist, elaborated upon this approach in a seminal book from 1976. *The Selfish Gene*[6] was in some ways a natural outgrowth of Darwin's ideas in that it incorporated his view of how evolution works with an extensive consideration of DNA, something that Darwin did not know about. Unfortunately, Dawkins went in a direction that some people found alienating. In the preface to the first edition of *The Selfish Gene*, for example, he wrote that "We are survival machines – robot vehicles blindly programmed to preserve the selfish molecules known as genes."[7] (Frankly, *we* are not amused.)

If you can get past its rhetorical excesses, *The Selfish Gene* is actually a very good book. It provides a clear, readable introduction to sociobiology. The excesses may be there because Dawkins was being facetious, but it does not read that way. *The Selfish Gene* seems dead-on serious, which is quite unfortunate because it seems to support two of the criticisms that are often leveled at sociobiology: that it is deterministic and reductionistic. The determinism seems patent in *The Selfish Gene*: "robots" that "blindly" follow the instructions of their DNA do not have much of a say in their future. It seems that Dawkins believes that we are bound to act out what is already in the cards for us, or in the genes in this case. Similarly, anyone who thinks that sociobiology is reductionistic is unlikely to be persuaded otherwise by *The Selfish Gene*. Could human behavior possibly be further reduced to insignificance? Maybe all this evolutionary theory is relevant for worker ants, but humans usually have a lot more going on than a simple urge to reproduce.

While sociobiology at its most extreme is nearly as nasty as its detractors say, its general principles are useful. The fact that some of its proponents are extremists is not a good excuse for dismissing the entire field. The rest of this chapter is an extended argument for the general relevance of these ideas to our lives – even though the course of human life and human behavior are not determined at birth, and even though people are much more than "robots" attempting to reproduce.

🦓　◉　◉　◉　🦓

Charles Darwin's ideas on evolution by natural selection provided the groundwork, then people like Robert Trivers, W.D. Hamilton, Richard Dawkins and E.O. Wilson, among others, elaborated upon Darwin's ideas, especially in relation to how evolutionary considerations affect behavior. In summary, sociobiology interprets and analyzes animal behavior as if genetic reproduction is the goal of an individual's life. Practitioners in this field tend to think in economic terms: what does something cost the individual in question, and what is she or he likely to gain from that action? How will various behaviors affect an individual's reproductive success? How do the costs and benefits balance out over time?

So, for example, if a sociobiologist observes a low ranking male baboon grooming a high ranking male baboon, the interpretation might be along these lines: nonhuman primates spend a lot of time picking through each other's fur cleaning and looking for parasites. Grooming a fellow baboon is a relatively low cost activity, unless the groomer is missing out on an opportunity to do something else of greater value (like find food or have sex). The benefit of spending time and energy grooming a high ranking male either might or might not be immediate. Even if there is not any immediate recompense (like learning from close up how the alpha male runs things), at some point in the future, the high ranking male might well remember kindly the youngster who spent all that time grooming him. Maybe someday the high ranking male will help the youngster rise in rank.

Sitting around picking through fur is a low cost activity, but sometimes animals are seen doing things that are much more expensive. It is rare, but occasionally individuals are even seen sustaining life threatening injuries in the course of defending their group. While this sort of thing might be seen as a challenge to the ideas of sociobiology, more than likely an individual that appears to be making that type of sacrifice is actually defending an investment. A male monkey, for example, who defends his group against another male who wants to join it might be doing so because the new male will kill any infants in the group he becomes a part of (this type of infanticide is not uncommon in primates). The first male monkey is protecting his own offspring and his opportunity to create more offspring in the future. He is protecting his own genetic immortality. The male who fights to keep another male out of his group is not doing so because of love or honor or any other abstract ideas – he is doing it because the kids in the group are his assets, and the females in the group represent his opportunity to reproduce.

Costs and benefits are thought of in terms of genetic reproduction. Again, siblings are related on average by ½ of their genes. Cousins also share genes, but fewer, approximately 1/8 in this case. Biologist J.B.S. Haldane once quipped that he would gladly lay down his life for three brothers or nine cousins.[8] Think about it for a moment: the three brothers would carry a total of 3/2 of his genes, and the cousins would altogether carry 9/8 of his genes. By sacrificing himself for three brothers or nine cousins, more copies of his own genes would survive than if he lived and all those family members did not.

The theories about the evolution of behavior described in this chapter have had a strong influence on biology in the past forty years or so, and there is fairly widespread agreement among biologists that this is the way evolution works. While I have mostly been discussing the theories, there is also plenty of empirical research that has been done by people who study animal behavior. Countless studies provide evidence from the natural world that Darwin was on to something when he suggested that evolution occurred by the process of natural selection.

Ironically, the success of this view of life has been criticized by some people because it is so far-reaching and because it does have such broad applicability. Harvard paleontologist and *Natural History* magazine columnist Stephen Jay Gould was one of sociobiology's most vocal critics.[9] Gould claimed that the field is "adaptationist,"[10] by which he meant that its practitioners think that every trait of every organism and every behavior of every animal is something that has been designed over the course of evolutionary time to help the individual in question reproduce. Sociobiology, according to some of its detractors, is nothing more than an opportunity to make up stories about evolution.

Gould and other critics do have a point. It is easy and fun to speculate on how things might evolve, especially if there is no way to test your ideas experimentally. For example, when I was teaching primate behavior to undergraduates, I rarely had teaching jitters because I knew that if anyone posed a question that I did not know the answer to I would be able to respond with a plausible prediction based on evolutionary theory. ("Why would that be the case? Let's consider some possibilities ....") And then I could look up the research after class.

Chance should be considered in discussions of evolution, and quite often it does not seem to be in sociobiology. Life is just too big and too messy to claim that its features are all "designed." Some things are just random, and some features of organisms are along for the ride, rather than being advantageous. One thing that is certain is that anything that is along for the ride should not *hurt* an organism's chance to reproduce. Deleterious stuff generally dies out quickly. Even if chance is a factor for particular individuals, evolutionary biologists are usually considering extremely long time frames over which randomness is less likely to have a great impact. If you play the lottery once in a while, you are unlikely to win. If you buy thousands of tickets over long periods of time, you are more likely (but still not guaranteed) to win.

Critiques notwithstanding, sociobiology is a thriving field with a large body of research that backs up Darwin's theory of evolution by natural selection. Sociobiology does have one significant problem though: just how applicable are these ideas to modern humans?

Many sociobiologists have subtle and nuanced perspectives on human behavior, but a few would say that the ideas described in Chapter Two and earlier in this chapter are *entirely* relevant to modern humans, and that no other perspective on human behavior even needs to be considered. I think of these people as the True Believers.

True Believers are like converts to a new religion. In the True Believer worldview, human behavior is no more complex than animal behavior. Cultural forces are irrelevant and genetic programming provides the impetus for what people do. Even though there is ample evidence that a broad variety of modern people do not act in ways that can be construed as attempts to "maximize their reproduction," a True Believer knows better: people are *subconsciously* in search of genetic immortality. That is the cornerstone of human behavior, even if much human behavior is only indirectly involved in reproduction. Even if it is convoluted, the True Believer will tell you that it is all about passing along those genes.

A True Believer's faith is not even shaken by something like birth control. Birth control to the True Believer mindset is a way to ensure that children will be born at the *right time* in their parents' lives. If a child is born at a time when the parents are not in a good position to care for and raise him, the costs might well outweigh the benefits. But when the timing is right for someone to have kids, birth control can be a way of arranging to give a child the best possible start in the competitive world into which he is brought. Among the True Believers, it goes without saying that everyone wants to have her or his own biological children. Of course some people use birth control to entirely avoid reproducing. This is harder to explain away, but things like this do not shake the faith of a True Believer.

Homosexuality is also a "problem" for True Believers. Having sex with others of the same sex is not a particularly good way to "maximize" reproduction. In fact if they exclusively have sex with people of the same sex, gay people will not reproduce at all. Some sociobiological suggestions about how homosexuality might have evolved will be discussed at greater length in Chapter Eight, in the context of a version of sociobiology that takes cultural variability into account and that also considers historical circumstances. Even though sociobiology has had a lack of success in explaining the existence of homosexuality, that does not invalidate the entire field. There is no reason to throw the evolutionary baby out with the bath water.

Unfortunately for sociobiology, it is often the True Believers who are quoted in the media. *New York Times* science writer Natalie Angier has referred to these people as the field's "hard-core" practitioners.[11] True Believers hold fast to their ideas in the face of strong evidence – even from their own lives – that contradicts the idea that people are trying to "maximize their reproduction." They hold fast even in the face of evidence that differences between men and women, rather than being strict and determined, do reflect and respond to changing cultural patterns.

Sociobiology is based on a few relatively simple and yet very powerful ideas that explain a great deal about how living things operate. These ideas are good ones and they are broadly applicable. These ideas explain a lot, but they do not explain everything about people. Not all human behavior is geared toward reproduction. There may have been a time in the evolutionary history of the human lineage when this was the case, but for all modern people – for all people alive today – life is more complex than the True Believers are willing to admit.

So what does an alternative soft-core sociobiology look like? I would suggest that soft-core sociobiology is the single best set of concepts that is available to explain what human beings typically do with their lives, at least in terms of how they relate to people around them. If you could possibly measure human behavior over the millennia and over all the world's cultures, you could come up with some averages that describe people. Note that I am not talking here about the *range* of humanity, but rather what are and have been typical behaviors that are engaged in by the vast majority of people. It would be impossible to actually measure these things, but the averages are important because they would be consistent with what sociobiology predicts about human behavior. The averages might well represent what we call human nature.

What are some things that might represent the typically human?[12] At the most basic level, people do want to survive and reproduce. This is not true for everyone, but I would suggest that it is very common. People also have an aversion to incest. Again, not all people, but a very large majority over all cultures. Historically, almost all people have married someone of the opposite sex. People are also generally interested in status – in being well thought of by others. Humans also typically live in groups. People tend to be willing to cooperate with others from their group, but they are more wary of others whom they do not know. Like other large-brained mammals, humans have reasoning abilities and use these abilities to keep track of shifting social situations. Humans form alliances, also like individuals from some other species. Much like the other territorial primates, humans seem to like to own things.

There are also average sex differences among humans. Across cultures, men are somewhat more enthusiastic about sex than women are, and men are somewhat more aggressive in general than women are. Cross-culturally, women, on the whole, are more nurturing; men are more proprietary, especially about women (why was it so easy for Iago to whip Othello into such a fit of sexual jealousy that he murders Desdemona?). Again, the ranges for these traits are wide, and vary from one culture to another, but I am talking about a *human average.*

All of these things are consistent with the predictions of evolutionary theory. All of these things are also continuous with the behavior of our closest relatives in nature, chimpanzees and gorillas, except that apes do not marry (though some, like gibbons, are monogamous). While it is conceivable that humans might be an entirely special case, the most parsimonious explanation for the averages is that sociobiology is on to something. The behavior of modern humans has much in common with that of apes. We may be quite different from chimpanzees, but the kinship is decidedly there, and to an extent the same principles of sociobiology apply.

The main difference between hard-core sociobiology and soft-core sociobiology is that the True Believers would leave the phrase "to an extent" out of the last sentence.

With evolutionary biology as a context, human behavior makes much more sense. While it is true that people are known to engage in a huge variety of behaviors, more often than not people from all the world's cultures do a lot of the same stuff over and over again. People can be astonishingly creative, but they usually aren't. Using the logical principle of Occam's razor – the simplest explanation is usually the best explanation – it is clear that the continuity of ape and human behavior derives from the same evolutionary processes. Does it make sense to think that every human culture independently invented, for example, an incest taboo? Or does it make more sense to suggest that incest avoidance is a deeply felt aspect of human nature? Animals avoid inbreeding without recourse to the cultural rules that humans have invented. But the end result is the same for humans and animals: individual infrequently mate with close relatives. Avoidance makes sense from an evolutionary perspective.

Perhaps it is reductionistic to consider the averages when the ranges of behavior are so interesting, but that does not make sociobiology either evil or incorrect. It is a different way of approaching the world than that of most of American social science, but it is a matter of perspective whether you choose to emphasize the differences among the world's people or the things that we all have in common. Emphasizing the differences does not seem to have advanced us very far in the direction of world peace and understanding so maybe it is time to consider the alternative. A century of cultural relativism in American social thought seems to have brought us to a point where many Americans understand that people are different because of cultural influences, but frankly they just don't care. Perhaps emphasizing a common humanity among all the world's people will make Americans less likely to drop bombs on people they do not like. Just a thought.

Soft-core sociobiology is not as reductionistic as hard-core sociobiology. While the latter form of this way of thinking might view humans and all other living things as reproducing machines, in soft-core sociobiology, reproduction is just one thing that motivates human behavior. It is an important item – most people do seem to want to reproduce – but it simply is not the case that humans are consistently trying to "maximize their reproduction," either consciously or subconsciously.

There are other things that motivate human behavior. For example, it is very common for people to be concerned with status, and with how they are viewed by others. For most of human evolution, higher status was probably correlated with greater reproduction. This would have been especially true for men because, as Trivers suggested, males are limited in their capacity to reproduce by the availability of fertile females. If the high status chief wanted to have sex with all the virgins in his group, he just might be able to do so. It is the *droit du seigneur*, the right of the master. Females, by contrast, have a potential to reproduce that is more limited than that of males. Even females of the highest status will not be able to give birth to more than one baby every year or so.

While an interest in status might formerly have been conducive to greater reproduction, the evolution of highly stratified societies in the past 10,000 years or so has frequently separated high status from concomitantly high reproduction. This is merciful in that recent world leaders, say American presidents from the latter half of the twentieth century for example, have had exorbitant power over very large groups of people. If it were still the case that status was proportionately correlated with reproduction, George H.W. Bush, for example, would have had infinitely more offspring than he did.

In the modern world, status brings its own rewards and more reproduction might or might not be among them. Greater access to sex probably is among the rewards of higher status. Throughout nearly all of human history, sex was closely correlated with reproduction. Only with the development of various birth control methods has it been possible for more sex not to be roughly equated with more offspring. At the beginning of the twenty-first century in America, more often than not sex happens for its own sake rather than because of an intention to procreate. More sex used to mean more babies, at least for men. Now it just means more sex.

Soft-core sociobiology does not consider people to be reproducing machines, even though viewing animal behavior from this perspective is compelling. If people can be likened to any kind of machine, we are more like reasoning machines that are nevertheless sometimes swayed by powerful emotions, the sources of which can remain rather obscure. Our technologies notwithstanding, at the beginning of the twenty-first century, we still have bodies and minds that are not substantially different from those of the first modern humans who lived between 50,000 and 100,000 years ago. It would be much too simplistic to say that there are genes "for" specific types of behavior. For example, there is no "gene for infidelity" that men have more often than women. But our brains are put together in such a way that we are predisposed to certain types of behaviors and emotions. Similarly, there is no single parenting gene that some people have (women?) and some people don't (men?). Rather, there is something akin to circuitry in the brain that has evolved over millions of years that predisposes people to certain types of behavior when they are confronted with a helpless baby. While care-giving behavior might be particularly easy to induce if the child is your own, almost any helpless crying baby that is all alone for whatever reason will cause a reaction in nearby adults. Given that humans probably evolved in small groups, this makes sense. For millions of years, more than likely a crying baby in the vicinity will either be yours or will belong to someone to whom you are related, either genetically or by marriage.

The metaphorical neural circuitry that predisposes adult humans to respond with care-giving and eventual attachment to a helpless baby is at the root of at least one type of behavior in American culture that seems almost inexplicable on its face: I am referring to the attachments that people form with their pets. Many people have extremely strong emotional connections with their pets. Even though we do not share too many genes with our cats and dogs, the care and love that people lavish on their pets uses the same neural circuitry that predisposes people to take care of their offspring. The death of a pet can be devastating, and while people might remind themselves at such a time that it was "only a dog" or "only a cat," the loss is no less traumatic. Rationality takes a back seat to the emotions.

Caring for a pet taps into the human predisposition to care for and bond with small, helpless beings. Because we evolved in small bands, humans are also predisposed to think in terms of group membership.[13] This has very broad implications. It was suggested earlier that it is a part of human nature to trust members of one's own group and to be wary of strangers. This type of behavior would have made sense during much of human evolution when small bands of people were likely to be competing against other groups of people for access to resources. This group-against-group mentality is ancient, and is something we share with the other primates, including our closest relatives, the chimpanzees and gorillas, other species that live in groups.

Brains of modern humans are set up in ways that reflect this evolutionary heritage. Again, I am not saying there is some kind of simplistic gene for xenophobia, but rather that the circuitry is such that people are predisposed to think in terms of us against them. It is really easy to invoke this type of mentality in modern humans.

To start with a fairly trivial example, think about sports in America. Many people, men in particular, have an extremely strong emotional response to sporting events. Often people are fanatically devoted to "their" team and their emotions rise and fall based on, for example, how the Red Sox are doing this year. Where does this devotion come from? Why are team sports a huge part of American culture? At a basic level, sports tap into the us against them brain circuitry that at one time was to our evolutionary advantage. Even though it is no longer a matter of survival, it is easy to evoke an interest in team sports because humans have brains that evolved in a context in which group membership was important.

A fanatical devotion to sports is relatively innocuous. However the us against them mentality that may have served our ancestors well is now unfortunately at the root of a widespread human tendency that is anything but innocuous. Through most of human history when people lived in small bands, it was probably relatively clear who was us and who was them. But now, especially in complex, stratified societies like twenty-first century America, defining us can be difficult. "We" can be Americans, and we can also be Red Sox fans, but it seems that we often define ourselves in terms of race, religion and ethnicity. The neural circuitry that was useful to our ancestors now probably also comes into play when people are taught to hate others who are different from them.

Racism and bigotry in general are all too common and all too easy to invoke in people because of the way our brains are set up. Humans rather naturally see unfamiliar others as suspicious. In societies that are more complex than small bands, young people have to be taught exactly who the others are. But human minds are predisposed to that way of thinking and people generally do not need too much convincing.

At the risk of taking this idea one giant step too far, I would suggest that the us versus them mentality is also at the root of the apparent twentieth century triumph of capitalism over communism. Capitalism thrives on free enterprise, which can be likened to teams (corporations) competing against other teams (corporations). Even if the corporations are large, if their employees can be convinced that they are a part of a team effort, corporations thrive and the self-interest of both the corporation and the employee is served. Their shared fate induces a level of cooperation between the individuals on the team. Communism tries to do this on a grand scale. But communism has run into trouble and in fact has failed spectacularly when the scale has been too grand. Even though people can learn how to cooperate with others in large-scale enterprises, human nature is such that people are still mostly concerned with themselves, their loved ones, and the people they know. Making a sacrifice in Minsk for a stranger in

Vladivostok is too obscure a concept. It is hard to imagine the stranger is really in your group or on your team. You really don't care about that person in Vladivostok.

In soft-core sociobiology, some behaviors are more natural than others. It isn't that people are hard-wired to do things like reproduce and hate strangers, but rather the structure of human neural wiring is conducive to certain types of behaviors. It is easier to convince people to do some things rather than others. Human nature is the equivalent of human tendencies that are elaborated upon and persuaded in various directions by cultures.

Some people still believe that human minds are a *tabula rasa*, or blank slate – a concept identified with English philosopher John Locke (1632-1704), whose thoughts were to be so influential among the founders of the American political system. Experiences and circumstances certainly do shape the behavior of the human animal. But the slate is not actually blank. While it might appear from a distance to be blank, if you look closely at it, you will notice that the slate has many grooves and channels cut into it. As experiences wash over the slate, it is easier for some ideas to be retained because they slip easily into the channels that a species' evolutionary history has etched into the slate over millions of years. The slate appears to be blank, but if you look at it closely – if you consider the third dimension – the human mind is an incised slate that can be more easily persuaded in some directions rather than others. This is not meant to imply that people are unable to change. The human species is highly adaptable, even if it has predispositions for certain behaviors.

For nearly all people alive today, our environments are very different from those in which humans evolved. For one thing, our social groups are huge compared with those of our ancestors, and these groups are often highly stratified. For another thing, many cultures rely upon elaborate technologies.

Prior to about 10,000 years ago, agriculture had yet to be developed. People lived in societies in which individuals had to hunt and gather all the food they were to consume. This was true for our ancestors; it is true for "traditional" societies and for our closest non-human relatives, the other apes. This was the world in which our brains and our emotions evolved. Soft-core sociobiology says that evolutionary considerations are important and that the same rules still apply – to a certain extent – to modern humans. But soft-core sociobiology also acknowledges that we are different from other animals.

There is often an implicit comparison of humans and other species in sociobiology. What about homosexuality? Is homosexual behavior seen in other species? The short answer is yes; homosexual behavior is seen fairly often in nature, especially in other primates. But human homosexuality differs in one very important way from the same-sex activity seen in other species. This is the topic of Chapter Four.

CHAPTER FOUR

Bisexual Monkeys

Baby, we can choose, you know we ain't no amoebas.
JOHN HIATT, "THING CALLED LOVE"

People who dislike gay people often explain their prejudice by resorting to the argument that homosexuality is unnatural. Radio talk show host and author Dr. Laura Schlessinger, for example, has referred to homosexuality as "deviant" and a "biological error."[1] Schlessinger, of course, is not alone in her opinion: it is rather widely believed that males and females are destined to mate with each other and have children. If God had meant for homosexuality to exist, so the tired old joke goes, he would have created Adam and Steve.

If we assume that unnatural means not found in nature, the idea that homosexuality is unnatural is incorrect in two ways. First of all, as a factual matter, homosexual behavior is *frequently* observed in species other than our own. Secondly, on a more philosophical level, it is simply wrong to equate "natural" with "good." People who do so cannot possibly know very much about the natural world. Biologists can tell you that there is quite a lot of sexual behavior between individuals of the same sex found in nature, and there are also a slew of other things that are perfectly "natural" that people either are generally offended by or have even outlawed. For example, in nature, our closest relatives are known to engage in rape, murder, and infanticide as well as some other practices that would be considered rather unsavory.

Human counterparts in nature are the nonhuman primates. They are so called to distinguish them from our species, because humans are also classified by scientists as primates. The human species, *Homo sapiens*, is very similar genetically, anatomically, physiologically and biochemically to the apes, or I should say, to the other apes, since people are classified as apes within the primate group. From a genetic perspective, we are just a few bits of DNA different from gorillas, chimpanzees, and orangutans. Our more distant relatives within the primate group include baboons, other types of monkeys, and a variety of rather exotic looking furry things called prosimians. Primates are distinguished from other mammals like rodents and carnivores by their tendencies toward larger brains, stereoscopic vision and grasping thumbs.

If we were to look to our closest nonhuman relatives in their natural habitats as role models for "natural" behavior, here are just a few of the more unappealing aspects of the lives of chimps, gorillas and orangutans that members of the human species have generally deemed criminal and/or disgusting.

Rape. Orangutans are large apes that live on the islands of Sumatra and Borneo where the eastern Indian Ocean meets the western Pacific. The name of the species is derived from a local phrase that is translated as "man of the forest," and indeed orangutans look like rather pudgy people who are covered with long red hair. Compared to most other primates, orangutans live a relatively solitary lifestyle. This is probably because they are very large and eat fruit – a *group* of orangs would have a hard time finding enough food in one patch of land, so individuals have to spread out to find enough to eat. The only orangutans who are seen together regularly are mothers and their young offspring.

Female orangutans seem to have a strong preference for mating with older males. From the perspective of the younger males, this is a problem, and the younger males of this species sometimes resolve this problem by forcibly mating with females. It is difficult to know what is on a female orangutan's mind, but it seems clear from observations in nature that the females do not want to mate with the younger males – they struggle, they attempt to escape, they put themselves at considerable risk to avoid mating with the younger males.[2] Since orang males are generally twice the size of the females, the struggle is often in vain.

In other words, rape is an aspect of "natural" behavior among orangutans. And orangs are not the only large-brained nonhuman species in which rape occurs. While people may think that dolphins are really cool, aggressive "herding" of females in heat by males has been described in at least one species of dolphin.[3] (Say it ain't so, Flipper!) In fact, sexual coercion of females by males is an extremely widespread "natural" occurrence.[4] Again, it is difficult for biologists who study animal behavior to know exactly what is on the minds of their subjects, but scientists often interpret female behavior as reluctant in terms of mating with particular males. The use of force or the threat of force is frequently how males overcome that reluctance. It is perfectly "natural."

Murder. It is well known that nature is a tough place – red in tooth and claw, eat or be eaten, etc. There is, however, a popular misconception that while animals may squabble among themselves like siblings, they do not kill their own kind. They kill – but only to eat. When they fight among themselves, it is believed, they stop short of intentionally murdering their own kind. Unfortunately this is not true. Those chimpanzees that look so cute on television and in the zoo can be cold-blooded killers.

Chimpanzees have been observed battering each other to death in the wild. Jane Goodall describes a pattern of attacks in her magnum opus that summarized the first quarter century of her research on chimpanzees at Gombe in Tanzania.[5] The killings are not one-on-one; rather they are lengthy gang attacks in which between two and five chimpanzees hit, stomp on, beat and drag around another chimp until the victim is incapacitated. Further, "all the victims were, at some point, held to the ground by one or more of the aggressors while the others hit and pounded."[6] Goodall's assistants who witnessed these attacks believed that the aggressors showed intent to kill. Like rape among the orangutans, murder is a "natural" part of the lives of chimpanzees.

Infanticide. Gorillas are large-bodied African apes. Unlike their Asian cousins the orangutans who eat fruit, gorilla diets are composed of quite a lot of vegetation and their environments are like one big salad bowl. Because they have less difficulty finding enough to eat than orangutans, gorillas are able to live in groups. In at least some areas, those groups consist of one adult male and a "harem" of unrelated females with whom he has offspring. Think about it for a moment: if a given population of gorillas has approximately as many males as females, and if one male has a number of females with whom he mates exclusively, then some other males will not have females to mate with at all. If one male has a harem of four or five females, then there are probably three or four other males who do not have females with whom to mate.

This "one-male group" type of social organization is not unusual among nonhuman primates. One side effect of this arrangement is that the adult males tend to fight among themselves for control of the groups of females. If a new male manages to displace a male from a group that he has been part of for some time, one of the first things the new male will try to do is kill the nursing offspring of the former harem owner.[7]

Why? The prevailing theory explaining this type of infanticide in nonhuman primates is that females whose nursing offspring are killed will stop lactating shortly thereafter and will soon start ovulating again. The new male then has an opportunity to mate with the females and have offspring of his own with them. In other words, the new male is not going to wait around and watch another male's kids grow up; instead he kills his rival's children and by doing so gains more time to reproduce his own version of primate genes, before he gets displaced.

Coprophagy. It is not easy to explain this politely. The word coprophagy is derived from a Greek word that, roughly translated, means shit-eating. While such an activity is the kind of thing that might be engaged in primarily by more primitive life forms like fungi and bugs, our close relatives are also known to engage in it. It is not unusual to see apes who have recently … had a good movement of the bowels … look through what they have produced in search of delectable morsels that did not get digested the first time through the gastrointestinal tract. If they find something to their liking, they will eat it and try again to digest it. No sense wasting delectable morsels.

Coprophagy is as natural as natural can be.

These are some of the more unsavory things engaged in by our closest relatives in the natural world, the apes with whom we share the majority of our DNA. These examples of "natural" behavior among our closest kin are generally subject to restrictive laws in a variety of human societies, or, in the case of coprophagy, considered to be disgusting.

Sociobiology reminds us that we are animals that have evolved over the past few million years; but, sociobiologists are also very aware that what is "natural" is not necessarily what is good. The ways of nature are not necessarily right. Nature is not always pretty.

It is not my intent here to class homosexuality with the unsavory. On the contrary, I am a big fan of homosexuality. Rather I am pointing out that people who argue that homosexuality is "unnatural" and who equate "natural" and "good" are profoundly ignorant of the ways of life on planet Earth. It is very hard to take a close look at animal behavior and believe that everything is for the best in this best of all possible worlds.[8]

Although nature should not be held up as a model for how best to live our lives, it is interesting from an evolutionary perspective that homosexual behavior is common in the lives of animals. Sociobiological theory is focused on how organisms are designed over the course of millions of years of evolutionary time to be virtual reproducing machines. Homosexual behavior is not uncommon in nature and yet it does not seem to serve any reproductive purpose. Why does it exist?

It is somewhat politically incorrect to ask this question. The politically correct perspective is something along the lines of "Since no one ever questions why heterosexuality exists, no one should question why homosexuality exists." Actually biologists do ask questions about heterosexuality and study reproduction and sexuality in all its forms. At the risk of being forced to give up my good liberal membership card, I am going to state the obvious. Heterosexuality is *rampant* in the natural world; it is generally how organisms reproduce themselves. When organisms do not reproduce heterosexually, they tend to be asexual and reproduce by doing rather unexciting things like dividing in half. It isn't easy to be homosexual and reproduce. It isn't impossible, but it isn't easy. In the context of evolutionary biology, homosexuality is a problem that needs to be explained.

There are two important questions that we have to examine. The first is what exactly do we mean when we are talking about homosexual behavior in organisms other than humans? The second question is to what extent is homosexual behavior observed in species besides our own?

The first question turns out to be both simple and quite complex. Even among humans defining homosexuality is not an easy task. Among animals, the question is made more difficult by our inability to know the intentions of the individuals involved. The simple answer to the question of how you define homosexual behavior in animals is that such behavior involves two or more individuals of the same biological sex who are engaging in an encounter involving the genitalia of at least one of the parties. This is the typical definition that is used by animal behaviorists when exploring the topic of same-sex sexuality in nonhumans.

This definition is simple enough on the surface, but made more complicated by the fact that an animal's desires are only inferred. For humans, homosexual behavior is generally homoerotic as well – it involves emotions and feelings. That might not be the case among nonhuman animals. It is quite possible that there is nothing "erotic" about sexual activity between members of the same sex of nonhuman species. Often, for example, when a monkey mounts another monkey of the same sex in a position much like that seen in heterosexual intercourse, the behavior may be little more than an expression of dominance with the more powerful animal on top. Mounting behavior is more of a message of "Hey, I'm in charge here," rather than "Hey, I think you're cute." Homosexual behavior is not necessarily homoerotic behavior.

Barring any astonishing new ways of gaining insight to the thought processes of other species, the definition of homosexual behavior given above will have to suffice when considering nonhuman animals. We do not know what the animals are thinking. It might be "Hey, I think you're cute," but there is a good chance that that is not what is being expressed in homosexual behavior.

The second question we need to consider is how extensively homosexual behavior is seen in species besides our own. The short answer is that there is quite a lot of same-sex behavior in the natural world, even though the natural world is a predominantly heterosexual place. Is it possible to quantify something like this? To say that nature is 95 percent or 99 percent heterosexual? No. Many animal species have not been studied at all and there would be no accurate way to estimate whether or not homosexual behavior would be seen in unstudied species. Even when it has been observed, it is still impossible to quantify. Would we be considering the number of individuals who (occasionally) engage in homosexual behavior? Or the number of times they do so? Would it be appropriate to compare numbers of same-sex contacts with opposite-sex contacts? We can only say with certainty that homosexual behavior is far from unknown outside the human species.

Even though it is predominantly heterosexual, nature is also a very varied and lively place. Among animal species that have been studied, variations on the theme of same-sex sexuality are regularly reported. Bruce Bagemihl did an exhaustive search of the scientific literature and his book *Biological Exuberance: Animal Homosexuality and Natural Diversity*[9] is over 700 pages long and catalogues perhaps every instance of nonhuman homosexual behavior that has been reported. It is encyclopedic. But you also get the impression that it is a book with an agenda. The author seems to want to put a gay-positive spin on the scientific literature. For example, Bagemihl includes grooming as a type of affectionate behavior seen in same-sex pairs, as well as simple huddling together of animals.[10] These hardly seem like homoerotic or homosexual activities. He also claims that "… homosexual parents are generally as good at parenting as heterosexual ones," and "some animals raise young in alternative family arrangements."[11] In a homophobic world where gay people are sometimes denied custody of their children, statements like these are probably meant to make people think that support for the concept of alternative family arrangements can be found in nature.

Is Bagemihl trying to show that homosexuality is "natural"? Possibly. He says, for example, "from the Southeastern Blueberry Bee of the United States to more than 130 different bird species worldwide, the 'birds and the bees,' literally, are queer."[12] And at least in some instances Bagemihl seems to be making leaps with the available data. For example, Bagemihl notes that "in those gibbon families where homosexual activity takes place, it occurs quite frequently."[13] Gibbons are a type of ape found in Southeast Asia and on nearby islands; these species have been studied in the wild and described in dozens of published articles, only one of which detailed an example of homosexual behavior in this group of species. The homosexual pairing was an extremely unusual father and son duo, and yet "Bagemihl describes male homosexual behaviour in white-handed gibbons ... as 'moderate' in terms of its importance in this species."[14] It might be true that as more gibbons are studied in the wild, more examples of homosexual behavior will be described. But then again that might not happen – the one reported case might well turn out to be an anomaly. Pending more data, homosexual behavior in gibbons seems to me to be significantly less important than Bagemihl implies.

If biologists are as heterosexually biased and homophobic as some people seem to think, it is hard to imagine that Bagemihl even would have been able to assemble the references that he did. It might be true that we do not have all the information we could on the topic of homosexual behavior in animals. This could be the case for a number of reasons. Homophobia on the part of some biologists is a possibility. Also, the dominant paradigm in evolutionary biology is that reproduction is the key to all things, and homosexual behavior seems puzzling from this perspective. It could be the case that homosexual behavior occurs so infrequently that it does not qualify as an academic MPU (a "minimal publishable unit"). Perhaps some homosexual behaviors are interpreted as dominance behaviors rather than sexual behaviors. It could also be true that people are reluctant to publish information on homosexuality because their funding sources or universities would be disturbed by their interest in the topic. Animal behaviorists do, however, have methods that are grounded in mathematics. In animal species that have been studied extensively, if homosexual behavior exists, it probably has been observed.

Given that they are our closest relatives, homosexual behavior among nonhuman primates is of particular interest.

Primatologist Paul Vasey has published a careful review of homosexual behavior in this group of mammals.[15] There are approximately 170 species of primates, some of which have not been observed in their natural habitats at all, and some of which have been studied intensively over the past forty years. The primate species most similar to our own – the common chimpanzee – has been studied in the wild by Jane Goodall and others since the early 1960s. Other species like various types of baboons have also been subject to extensive, long-term research. How much homosexual behavior has been observed?

Vasey's review found that homosexual behavior has been described in 33 species of primates. Because some species have not been studied yet, or have not been studied very intensively, it seems likely that that number will grow somewhat in the future. Interestingly, all 33 of the primate species in which homosexual behavior has been observed are classified among the "higher" primates – that is, animals that have relatively larger brains and more complex social development. (Humans are classed among the higher primates, which is not surprising given that one of us made up the terminology.) Homosexual behavior has not been observed at all among the prosimians, or lower primates. One aspect of the social behavior of the higher primates is increased behavioral flexibility and, according to Vasey, "the decoupling of sexual behavior from mere reproduction."[16]

Vasey also found that "in the vast majority of cases, homosexual behavior reflects a normal facet of the sexual repertoire of primates ...."[17] Primate sexual repertoires generally are quite flexible, and the frequency with which homosexual behavior is observed is variable. In some species, it seems to be completely absent whereas in others homosexual behavior reaches levels that "approach or even surpass heterosexual behavior."[18] Vasey divided species into three categories depending on whether homosexual behavior had been observed rarely, occasionally or frequently. In about half of the species in which it occurs, homosexual behavior is rare, but in the other half, it is either frequent or at least occasional. Moderate numbers of both males and females engage in homosexual behavior. Vasey defined homosexual behavior as "genital contact, genital manipulation or both between same-sex individuals."[19]

Groups of primates are organized in a number of different ways. For example, gorillas are often seen in "one-male" groups in which one male is in association with a number of unrelated females. Chimpanzees are found in groups that contain many males and many females. Some species, like gibbons, are found in monogamous "family" units (mom, dad and the kids), and solitary individuals with overlapping ranges are also known (orangutans). Homosexual behavior has been seen in all the different types of groups, but more commonly in groups in which many females live with many males.[20] Species organized this way may just generally have all kinds of sex more frequently than in other types of social groupings. Homosexual behavior also seems to be common in the all male groups that sometimes form when single males control the movements of groups of females. While you might predict that homosexual behavior would also be common in all female groups, nonhuman primates are rarely found in such groups. Female nonhuman primates will almost always have males hovering about.

Hovering males do not deter the females of at least one species from expressing their fondness for each other. The bonobo, or pygmy chimpanzee, is a close cousin to the more well known common chimpanzee studied by Jane Goodall. Bonobos have not been studied in the wild for as long as common chimps, and it is only since the 1980s that there have been books and a number of articles published on this species.[21] Bonobos live in the Congo (formerly Zaire) in central Africa. Their dense jungle habitat makes this a difficult species to study in their natural environment, but a number of primatologists have made the effort, and the results are very interesting. Generally, bonobos seem to be quite a bit nicer than their common chimpanzee cousins. Like common chimps, the social groups in which these animals live are made up of a number of males and a number of females. Also as in common chimps, the males tend to be related to each other whereas the females are unrelated and have transferred into the group from other groups.

Why is one sex related and the other not? In most groups of mammals, at least one of the sexes disperses from the group in which it was born. This has probably evolved over millions of years as a way of minimizing the risk of inbreeding. If a group of animals has a territory on which it lives, it will likely be the case that either the males or the females leave the territory upon reaching adulthood. In both bonobos and common chimpanzees, the females leave the groups they were born into and move into new groups when they are ready to mate and start having offspring. By doing this they basically ensure that they will not mate with their fathers or brothers or any other close relatives.

Having to move into a new group does not make for a great situation for common chimpanzee females. In other species (like most monkeys) where males move at puberty, the females form the core of the primate society. Kin groups in these species revolve around sisters and mothers and nieces, and the males are transitory. But the unfortunate female chimps are in groups without the natural allies created by kinship and long familiarity. For common chimp females, life is pretty lonely. Their bonobo cousins, however, have developed quite an interesting way to bond with unrelated females in the groups they move into. They have sex with each other. Lots of it.

Sex among female bonobos deserves a full description:

> "Perhaps the bonobo's most typical sexual pattern, undocumented in any other primate, is genito-

genital rubbing (or GG rubbing) between adult females. One female facing another clings with arms and legs to a partner that, standing on both hands and feet, lifts her off the ground. The two females then rub their genital swellings laterally together, emitting grins and squeals that probably reflect orgasmic experiences."[22]

How are these interactions arranged?

"The following is a typical example. First, female A approaches female B, who is in the midst of feeding. Female A, who approached in an unconcerned manner, lingers a bit and sits down at a distance, but within easy reach of B …. A stands bipedally, extends her hand to B, puts her face close to B's face, and peers directly at her …. If B does not react, A may grasp B's knees with her feet, or some other body part, and shake her. Alternatively, A may touch B's shoulder and peer at B in a request. These are all requests that say, 'Please associate with me in genital rubbing.' Then, B rolls over on her back and spreads her thighs."[23]

Female bonobos also have quite a lot of sex with males, and males sometimes have sex with each other, but the female-female sexuality is a particularly noticeable aspect of sexual repertoire of this species. While it can occur at any time, sex between female bonobos frequently occurs when a female is first moving into a new group[24] – almost as if an old-timer is welcoming her and showing her the ropes. (I believe this is a staple plot line in women's prison movies as well.) The females also rather inexplicably tend to have sex with each other when they discover a new and exciting source of food in their patch of forest.

Primatologists cannot know what their subjects are thinking. Based solely on observations of their behavior, however, it looks like female bonobos are really enjoying themselves. If every species had a theme song, the bonobo tune would probably be "Girls Just Wanna Have Fun" (apologies to Cyndi Lauper).

In summary, in the nonhuman primates, homosexual behavior has been observed in some species and not in others. *Within* particular species, some individuals have been observed engaging in homosexual behavior and others have not. But there is an important way in which homosexual behavior in nonhuman primates differs from what is seen among humans. Nonhuman primates who engage in homosexual behavior also engage in heterosexual behavior. If there are significant exceptions to this, they have yet to be seen in nature.[25] To use human terms, our monkey and ape cousins tend to be bisexual when they are not heterosexual.[26] In naturally reproducing species in their natural environment, there is little evidence that there are any nonhuman primates that are oriented toward having sex exclusively with other individuals of the same biological sex.

When exclusive homosexual behavior is seen in species other than our own, it is often in the context of conditions that are unusual for some reason. So, for example, I make very little of the extensive homosexual behavior reportedly seen in some domesticated and zoo animals. Animals such as these often live in situations that are quite different from the natural conditions that their relatives experience in the wild. With captivity and domestication come demographics unlike those seen in nature. If a captive group of animals contains an abundance of males, it should not be a surprise if there is sexual activity among the males. At most, homosexual behavior in captive and domestic animals indicates a bisexual capacity that may be present in many living things.

Exclusive homosexual orientation is occasionally seen in some kinds of animals in the wild, but it is usually in the context of a skewed sex ratio – there are many more males than females, or vice versa, and the extra members of the over-represented sex pair up with each other. On those rare occasions when they are seen in nature, exclusive homosexual pairings tend to occur when the option of heterosexual pairings is ruled out – like in prisons or the military or Catholic schools among *Homo sapiens*.

The apparent absence of an exclusive homosexual orientation in nonhuman primates and other species is important because it means that individuals in their natural environments that are engaging in homosexual behavior are not likely to completely forego reproduction. If sexual contact is *exclusively* with others of the same sex, reproduction is impossible. But if an individual has sexual contact with both males and females, that individual might well reproduce. Bisexuality is less of an evolutionary conundrum than homosexuality since individuals are still likely to have offspring.

Even though it is less of an evolutionary mystery, bisexuality is still something of a "problem" from the perspective of evolutionary biology, because having sex with another individual of the same biological sex clearly will not result in reproduction. It does not seem, on its face, to be likely to enhance reproduction in any way. And it is a costly activity in that the individuals engaging in it, theoretically at least, could be spending their time and energy doing things that are more directly related to survival and reproduction. In some species, at least some individuals spend a lot of time and energy arranging and then experiencing homosexual encounters. *Any* homosexual behavior, if you want to be strict about it, seems like a "waste" of time and energy, and yet it is seen fairly often in nature. If organisms have been designed over the course of millions of years to reproduce as much as possible, anything that detracts from that goal, in theory at least, should not stay around.

Why is homosexual behavior seen among our nonhuman kin? Sociobiologists have suggested a number of what are termed functional explanations for the existence of homosexual behavior in nonhuman animals. They are called functional explanations because they posit that the behavior in question has some kind of function that is related – probably in the long term – to reproduction.

One very cogent suggestion about the evolution of the extravagant sexuality seen in bonobos was made by Harvard primatologist Richard Wrangham. Wrangham suggested that in bonobos, sex had evolved communication functions.[27] "Communication sex," Wrangham suggested, is seen in three main contexts. First of all, it is used to develop social relationships. This is seen particularly in the adult female bonobos who bond with each other in ways that common chimpanzee females do not. Secondly, communication sex is used sometimes in situations where aggression is a possibility, but sexual activity quells the urge to fight. Thirdly, sex in bonobos is used to repair social relationships after aggressive incidents.[28] All that sex might well be what makes bonobos seem nicer than their cousins the common chimpanzees.

More generally, same-sex sexuality can function in nonhuman primates to bond individuals together, cement alliances, form social networks, assist individuals in the obtaining of food or other resources, and possibly even in the avoidance of predators. All of these things may not directly result in reproduction, but it is conceivable that they might enhance an individual's chances of surviving and – over the long term – reproducing.

And besides that, it's fun too.

So, for example, female bonobos have sex with each other because it is a way of ensuring that a newcomer will become a part of the community and ally herself with the other females. These alliances are potentially useful to both the new arrivals and the females who welcome them to the group. There is a possibility that these alliances will somehow enhance reproduction for the individuals involved. The fact that the female bonobos have sex with each other when they find a large food patch is a bit more difficult to explain from a functional perspective.

Sociobiologists tend to think long term. It seems quite obvious to the casual observer that female bonobos are having sex with each other because it is fun, but fun is not a very scientific explanation. It is also short term. Will homosexual behavior somehow enhance their reproduction in the long term? That is the kind of thing sociobiologists expect to find.

Scientists do not usually consider non-functional explanations, but I personally think it is time to put the fun back into functional explanations. Sex has evolved to be enjoyable for large-brained creatures like primates. Some of them have sex a lot, and only a tiny percentage of their sexual encounters are likely to lead to conception and the evolutionarily important increased reproductive success. But sexual behavior that cannot possibly result in offspring is still a significant part of the animals' repertoire.

Homosexual behavior is just one aspect of the sexual behavior of nonhuman primates that does not seem directly to enhance their reproduction. At least among some primates, there is also heterosexual activity well in excess of anything that would be necessary for conception. In addition to this overabundance of heterosexual behavior, there is also quite a lot of sexual behavior between juveniles, and between juveniles and adults. (It's perfectly "natural"!) Thus, homosexual behavior is not the only type of sexual behavior that does not seem to be directly enhancing fitness or contributing toward maximizing reproduction. There is a lot of sexual behavior among our nonhuman primate cousins that has little if anything to do directly with reproduction. Sexuality that goes well beyond what is strictly necessary for reproductive purposes is like an insurance policy. A vast enjoyment of sexuality, while it seems like a waste of energy from a very strict evolutionary perspective, has worked well for species like ours, and for the bonobos. Reproduction is virtually assured because sex is fun.

What can we conclude? While evolutionary theory might predict that organisms are designed to be efficient reproducing machines, in fact, there is some play in the system. The machines are not as ruthlessly efficient as you might expect.

Some practitioners in sociobiology have a tendency to go too far when they invoke evolutionary ideas to explain behavior. Living beings are diverse and things are not always as straightforward as sociobiologists would like them to be. There is a lot of non-reproductive sex going on in nature, and sociobiologists have not focused on it enough, probably because it does not fit in well with the general paradigm in which reproduction must be maximized. For some individuals and even some species, non-reproductive sexual behavior represents the expenditure of a lot of time and energy, as well as time lost in terms of feeding, and opportunities missed in terms of social maneuvering. To sociobiologists who are used to looking at life in terms of costs and benefits, all that sex that will not result in offspring costs a lot and results in little in the way of benefits. And yet non-reproductive sex is common, at least among some species.

Clearly, the evolutionary paradigm has great explanatory power but its interpretation needs to be loosened up a bit. At least among the larger-brained animal species (ourselves included), sex is not just for reproduction.

Nonhuman primates have been studied in the wild only since the early 1960s. It is often quite difficult to study monkeys and apes in their natural habitats, and consequently the number of individuals studied intensively is limited. It is possible that there are individual nonhuman primates who are sexually active by choice only with others of the same biological sex. Possible, but not likely. Exclusive homosexuality is seen only infrequently in nature, and then almost always in a context in which there are many more males than females or females than males. It may be the case that the human species is the only species on Earth in which some individuals are entirely sexually oriented toward individuals of the same biological sex.

Even though primate societies exert an influence on monkeys and apes, nonhuman primates do not have the same types of social constraints that humans do. For example, there is no reason to think that there is homophobia among our close kin. If a male chimpanzee or gorilla or orangutan never wanted to have sex with a female of his species, but instead only wanted to have sex with other males, there isn't anyone to stop him (barring perhaps the objections of those other males). This is very different from the situation among humans, in that nonhuman primates would never hear anything like "You'll go to hell," or "Please don't, it would kill your father," or "You wanna what? that's sick!" Yet as far as primatologists know, no male monkeys or apes are exclusively sexually oriented towards other males.

The case for female nonhuman primates is more complicated. Because of the likelihood that females can be sexually coerced by males, if there were female monkeys or apes that were exclusively sexually oriented toward other females, the possibility that these individuals would be able to follow their inclinations is slight at best. A female chimp that had no interest in sex with male chimps probably would not have much of a choice in the matter since sexual coercion is a significant aspect of the lives of many female nonhuman primates.[29] (There are parallels to this situation among humans that will be discussed in Chapter Seven.)

If there were a simple gene for homosexuality among nonhuman primates – a strip of DNA that somehow produced an invariable sexual orientation toward others of the same biological sex – then there would be "gay" monkeys and apes. Their fellow nonhuman primates would not discriminate against them. This is not necessarily the case among humans. If some humans have a gene for homosexuality that invariably produces a sexual orientation toward others of the same biological sex, the people who have that gene might or might not be able to fulfill their genetic predisposition because of societal constraints. The laws, rules and norms that are such a significant part of human cultures might prevent a person with a gene for homosexuality from fulfilling her or his sexual predilection.

Despite homophobia, and despite the existence of social constraints on the expression of same-sex eroticism among humans, some people are thoroughly gay. Some lesbians and gay men believe that they were "born that way" because they knew that they were different from other children very early in their lives – before they even knew of the existence of something called homosexuality. If there is a gene for homosexuality, the human species might be the only species that has it. The evidence that there is a biological basis for homosexuality in humans will be considered in Chapter Five.

CHAPTER FIVE

Hereditary Homosexuality

Would it be natural? ... This love suggests there is something beyond self-interest. The geneticists will scoff and since I cannot prove them wrong any more than they can prove themselves right, I shall only mention that scoffing is not a very scientific approach.

JEANETTE WINTERSON, GUT SYMMETRIES[1]

The most important thing to know about the biology of homosexuality is that the amount of media coverage is wildly out of proportion to the amount of actual science involved.

As a general rule, most scientists toil away in obscurity. They publish numerous papers and, maybe once in a lifetime, their work makes it into the Science section of the *New York Times*. A lifetime of research, fifteen minutes of something akin to fame. This situation is probably just fine with most researchers as their usual audience is made up of their students and their fellow scientists. But some topics are hotter than others – some topics are much more likely to catch people's attention. A biological basis for sexual orientation is one of those topics. Everybody wants to hear about this. A mention in the Science section? Heck, if you do research on sexual orientation, you could wind up on *Nightline*.

Why are people so interested in this topic? A partial answer to this question is that many people, both straight and gay, seem to find it reassuring to think that sexual orientation is something that is determined by biology. Gay people are reassured because they can argue that it is wrong to face discrimination because of something that cannot be changed and "just can't be helped." Straight people are reassured because the fact that they have only been attracted to people of the opposite sex is deeply rooted in their beings. It isn't that they are narrow-minded, homophobic or unimaginative. They are just straight and that is that. (I suspect that scientific studies that show biological differences between straight and gay people are utterly maddening to people who consider themselves to be bisexual. But that is another story. Or two.)

I will return to the topic of the zeitgeist of sexual orientation research later in this chapter. For now, what is the scientific evidence that lesbians and gay men are biologically different from heterosexuals? The issue is far from definitively settled, but some interesting work has been published which suggests that differences might exist.

Research on the biology of sexual orientation can be grouped into four broad categories: (1) neuroanatomical studies, (2) family and sibling studies, (3) DNA studies, and (4) miscellaneous research.

(1) Neuroanatomical studies

Are gay men and lesbians born that way? In 1991, the nature side of the nature/nurture debate as it applies to sexual orientation got a big boost with the publication of a brief paper by neurobiologist Simon LeVay in the prestigious journal *Science*.[2] Much media coverage ensued.[3] LeVay, who is openly gay, had previously done research on vision, but the paper that made him famous was on a brain difference between straight and gay men. More specifically, LeVay found that a section of the hypothalamus of straight men was twice as large as the corresponding area of the brains of gay men.

What is the hypothalamus and why would someone look there in particular to see if gay men were anatomically different from straight men?

The hypothalamus is a section of the brain found under ("hypo") the thalamus. It is a small structure located approximately in the middle of the brain. It is connected to and controls the pituitary gland which itself is a kind of master gland that influences other glands. The hypothalamus more or less regulates the body's internal environment, influencing things like hunger, thirst, temperature, blood pressure and some sexual functions.[4] LeVay was interested in a particular section of the hypothalamus because "this region of the brain is believed to be involved in the regulation of male-typical sexual behavior."[5] More specifically, the third interstitial nucleus of the anterior hypothalamus ("INAH3") had been shown by other researchers to be larger in men than in women. LeVay hypothesized that this section of the brain might also vary with sexual orientation.

LeVay assembled a collection of brain tissue from 41 autopsies. Nineteen of the brains were from gay men; sixteen of them were from straight men and the remaining six brains were from women who were assumed to be heterosexual. LeVay was unable to obtain brain tissue from women who could be confirmed to be lesbians (although it is interesting to speculate about what he might have found if he had). LeVay's work on the brain tissue was "blind" meaning that he did not know the sex or sexual orientation of the individuals from whom the samples were taken while he studied them.

> "… LeVay cut each hypothalamus into serial slices, stained these to mark the neuronal cell groups and measured their cross-sectional areas under a microscope. Armed with information about the areas, plus the thickness of the slices, he could readily calculate the volumes of each cell group."[6]

It was painstaking work: "at its largest, the human INAH3 constitutes approximately .000009 percent of the brain's mass."[7]

What did LeVay find? First of all, his research confirmed the earlier report that INAH3 was twice as large in heterosexual men than in presumed heterosexual women. But then came the really newsworthy item: LeVay also found that INAH3 varied in men according to sexual orientation, with the brains of gay men being more similar to the brains of women as far as that section of the hypothalamus was concerned. "In the gay men INAH3 was on average the same size as in the women, and two to three times smaller than in the straight men."[8]

LeVay's work was not without its critics. The first point on which the research was vulnerable was that all of the gay men whose brains were studied had died of complications of AIDS, and it is possible that LeVay's findings reflected changes in the brain wrought by HIV infection. While this cannot be ruled out entirely, six of the straight men had also died of AIDS complications (as had one of the women). Secondly, as LeVay himself noted, the differences he reported between straight and gay men were averages, and "some of the women and gay men had a large INAH3, and some of the presumed heterosexual men had a small one."[9]

Another study of the anterior hypothalamus by a different team of researchers found that "there was a trend for INAH3 to occupy a smaller volume in homosexual men than in heterosexual men, [but] there was no difference in the number of neurons within the nucleus based on sexual orientation."[10] In other words, gay men tended to have the same number of cells in that area of the brain, but the cells themselves were smaller and thus took up less space than the larger, heterosexual brain cells. Interestingly, researchers at the Oregon Health & Science University School of Medicine have found that the brains of male sheep also vary depending on whether a particular animal preferentially mates with females or with other males.[11]

What can be concluded from this line of research? The findings of brain differences between some gay men and some straight men certainly should not be taken as proof that gay men are born that way, but the implication is that it is possible that that might be the case. Other neuroanatomical studies have also pointed in the same direction.[12] The take away point is that some structural differences have been found between the brains of straight and gay men. At least in the hypothalamus, size apparently does matter.

(2) Family and sibling studies

As mentioned, 1991 was a big year for the nature side of the nature/nurture debate as it swirls around the topic of sexual orientation. In addition to Simon LeVay's paper on a brain difference between straight and gay men, a paper was also published by Northwestern University psychologist J. Michael Bailey and Boston University psychiatrist Richard Pillard that suggested that genes play a strong role in the development of homosexuality in men.[13] Two years later, Bailey, Pillard and two of their colleagues published a similar study that suggested that sexual orientation in women is also influenced by genetics.[14]

Before looking more specifically at Bailey and Pillard's findings, it might be useful to briefly consider the rationale behind the type of research they conducted.

Recently there has been a greatly expanded interest in the field of behavioral genetics, an area that focuses, as its name suggests, on the genetics of various types of behavior. It is a field whose practitioners seem to be considering the relative influence of nature and nurture on behavior, but who are in fact primarily interested in the influence of genes. Sociocultural factors are considerably less important than genetic factors in this paradigm. Studies in behavioral genetics sometimes look simply at how traits run in families and infer genetic influence from the patterns that are found. Other studies in behavioral genetics look at actual DNA in order to find specific segments of chromosomes that might include a gene for the trait of interest. Both of these types of study are fraught with potential problems. In family studies, for example, traits may be found to run in families, but families are also notorious for sharing similar environments. DNA studies may show the common existence of particular segments of DNA in people who share the trait of interest, but it is a huge developmental leap from correlation to causality. Two individuals might have similar genes but can those genes be shown to have actually *caused* the trait of interest? Not very often.

Within the field of behavioral genetics, studies of twins and other siblings have become particularly popular in recent decades.[15] Twins are of two varieties: they are either the result of the splitting of a single fertilized egg, in which case they are genetically identical to each other, or they are the result of two separate fertilized eggs that happen to gestate at the same time. In this case the twins are referred to as fraternal; they are genetically no more similar to each other than any other pair of siblings (full siblings generally share 50% of the same genes). Identical twins are also referred to as monozygotic ("mono" or one zygote or fertilized egg) and fraternal twins are also known as dizygotic ("di" or two zygotes or fertilized eggs).

If a trait is entirely determined by a gene – a particular segment of DNA – then you would expect that identical twins would both exhibit the trait since the twins have exactly the same DNA. How often, if one identical twin is gay, is the other gay as well? If a trait is determined by environment, then an identical twin of a gay sibling would have no more likelihood of themselves being gay than any other sibling. Fraternal twins are often raised in essentially the same environment, but unlike identical twins they are no more genetically similar than any other siblings. How often are two fraternal twins gay?

Michael Bailey and Richard Pillard recruited lesbians and gay men for their studies using ads in gay publications. They advertised that they wanted to talk to lesbian, gay or bisexual adults who had either a same-sex twin or an adopted sibling of the same sex. People who responded to the ads were interviewed and then questionnaires were sent to their siblings. In the 1991 study of gay men, Bailey and Pillard found that 52% of their monozygotic twins, 22% of dizygotic twins, and 11% of adoptive brothers were gay. In the 1993 lesbian study, Bailey et al. found that 48% of monozygotic twins, 16% of dizygotic twins, and 6% of adoptive sisters of lesbians were also lesbians.

Bailey and Pillard's findings suggest that there is a genetic influence in the development of homosexuality. This is consistent with other studies of homosexuality in twins,[16] as well as with other studies by Bailey, Pillard and their colleagues that more generally show that homosexuality runs in families.[17] Gay people seem to be more likely to have gay siblings than you would expect given the prevalence of homosexuality in the population at large. If one member of a pair of identical twins is gay, the chances are quite good that the other twin will be gay as well. In particular, the Bailey and Pillard twin studies show that there is a difference between twins who share exactly the same genes and twins who do not share exactly the same genetic material. Based on this information, you could argue that there is a substantial genetic influence on homosexuality.

On the other hand, you could also say that these studies suggest that there is a substantial environmental influence on homosexuality. If homosexuality was determined by a simple gene, then it should *always* be the case that if one monozygotic twin is gay then the other one should be as well. But that is not always the case – in fact it is only true around half the time. The interpretation of these studies depends on your perspective; they can be spun either as evidence supporting a genetic influence on homosexuality or as evidence against simple genetic causation and in favor of environmental influence.

In fact, these family studies of homosexuality tend to support the idea that a complex behavioral trait like sexual orientation is likely to be the result of an interaction of both nature (genes) and nurture (environment). Although the dichotomy of nature *or* nurture is common, it is not particularly accurate or enlightening. Living things always develop in some type of environment. Complex behavioral traits are likely to be influenced by constellations of genes that interact with each other in developmentally unique environments. It is a complicated world.

(3) DNA studies

Studies in behavioral genetics usually look at either family patterns in certain traits or at the actual DNA of individuals who exhibit the trait of interest. Studies by Dean Hamer and his colleagues at the National Institutes of Health have investigated both family patterns of homosexuality as well as the actual DNA of their subjects.[18] Hamer's findings received a huge amount of media attention when his first major study on this topic was published in the summer of 1993.[19] Hamer's team found that pairs of gay brothers shared a section of a chromosome more often than would be predicted by chance. Could this be a gay gene?

This investigation into whether or not male sexual orientation is genetically influenced began by recruiting a number of gay men through gay publications and an outpatient HIV clinic. The first step in the project was to get detailed information about the biological families of the participants in the study. This information was assembled into family trees that indicated which family members were known to be homosexual. There were 114 families that participated in this portion of the study, and the results of the pedigree analysis showed that gay men were pretty likely to have gay brothers, and they were also likely to have other gay male relatives on their mother's side of the family. There were more maternal uncles who were gay and more gay male cousins on the mother's side of the family than you would expect given the percentage of the general population that is made up of homosexuals. (One of the critiques of Hamer's study was that their results depended to a certain extent on the background rate of homosexuality in the general population. Hamer's team estimated that gay men make up 2% of the population. If they had used a higher number – as some studies indicate perhaps they should have – then their results would not have achieved statistical significance.[20])

Implicit in the finding that there were more gay male relatives on the female side of the families under investigation was the possibility that homosexuality was being passed on through the mothers' genes. (Shortly after Hamer's study was published some gay men started sporting t-shirts that said "Thanks for the genes Mom.") As Hamer et al. explained,

> "One explanation for the maternal transmission of a male-limited trait is X chromosome linkage. Since males receive their single X chromosome exclusively from their mothers, any trait that is influenced by an X-linked gene will be preferentially passed through the mother's side of the family."[21]

The next step in the research was to look at the X chromosomes of gay men to see if they shared genes on that chromosome. Hamer's team recruited a total of 40 families in which there were two gay brothers and little evidence that homosexuality was present on their father's side of the family tree. Hamer's team hypothesized that such families would be "enriched for the putative maternally transmitted genetic factor and therefore display further increases in the rates of homosexuality in maternally derived uncles and male cousins."[22] In other words, Hamer and his colleagues carefully chose subjects whose family trees indicated that they would be likely to fit the genetic pattern they were interested in. The gay men included in this study were not a random group.

An aside about human DNA: in addition to 22 pairs of general chromosomes, humans also have one pair of sex chromosomes that determine whether an individual is female or male. Females have two X chromosomes (one from each of her parents) and males have one X and one Y chromosome. Mothers will pass one of their two X chromosomes on to each of their sons while fathers will pass their one Y chromosome on to each of their sons.

The DNA analysis performed by Hamer's team on the pairs of gay brothers showed that the brothers had inherited the same X chromosome from their mothers in 33 of the 40 pairs. This was more than would be expected by chance, and in fact a particular region of the X chromosome, known as Xq28, was very similar in the pairs of gay brothers. Hamer used this result to argue that "at least one subtype of male sexual orientation is genetically influenced."[23] The study was rather cautiously worded and it did not conclude that there is a single gene which determines that its bearer will be attracted to people of the same sex. However, the implication in this work is that there is at least some genetic influence on some forms of homosexual behavior.

Two years after the original gay gene study, Hamer's team published a second study that more or less confirmed their original research,[24] but another group of researchers has failed to replicate their results.[25] Even if this work is replicated in the future by other scientists, a connection between this section of the X chromosome and sexual orientation is not necessarily one of causality. There could just be a correlation between a particular DNA pattern in this area and homosexuality. It is not inconceivable for example that the gene that has been found by Hamer's team is one that inspires people to volunteer for genetic studies.

Hamer's group was looking at a specific type of family in which gay men appear on the mothers' side of the family tree more often than one would expect by chance. DNA analysis was done on a very particular subset of the gay population of the United States: pairs of gay brothers whose family histories suggested that there might be maternal transmission of the trait in question. There are many gay men who do not have family histories that are similar to those of the 40 pairs of gay brothers.

As noted, the development of sexual orientation is likely to be a complex process that is influenced by a suite of genes as well as important environmental considerations. While the research described here is an interesting intimation that there might be a gay gene, the point has hardly been proven.

(4) Miscellaneous research

With all due respect to the scientists involved, this category of miscellaneous research on the biology of homosexuality includes some studies that appear, on the surface, to be rather bizarre in both conception and results. Why, for example, would someone look at finger length to explore sexual orientation? Why would someone else look at fingerprints? Why would yet someone else be looking at clicking sounds made by a portion of the inner ear? Why would people even think to look for such differences? The short answer to this question is that these physical differences are thought to correspond in some way with sexuality. In other words, these traits might underlie other traits that are less easily explored. So, for example, if some aspect of the hearing of gay people is measurably different from that of straight people, those differences might reflect neuroanatomical differences which might themselves reflect genetic differences. Gay people might indeed have been born that way.

In the case of the fingerprint study, for example, Jeffrey Hall and Doreen Kimura at the University of Western Ontario found that 30% of the gay men in their study had more fingerprint ridges on their left index fingers and thumbs than on their right. This pattern was found in only 14% of the straight men in the study.[26] Kimura "speculates that there is a link between finger ridge patterns and the development of the nervous system."[27] Since fingerprints are established in utero, differences in fingerprints between straight and gay men might quite literally been something that they were born with.

In 1998, Dennis McFadden and Edward Pasanen from the University of Texas published a paper in which they showed that lesbian ears (the ears of lesbians that is) responded to a weak clicking sound in a way that was more like the response of straight men than straight women.[28] Since male-female differences in this area have been shown to exist even in very young children, the researchers speculated that the differences between lesbians and straight women they found might have arisen due to differing exposure to prenatal androgens or male sex hormones.

The idea that prenatal androgens might be at the root of differences between adult heterosexuals and homosexuals was also the incentive for a study that looked at finger length ratios. Marc Breedlove and colleagues at the University of California at Berkeley surveyed 720 adults who were attending street fairs in the San Francisco area.[29] It had previously been shown that in women, the index finger is usually around the same length as the ring finger, whereas in men, the index finger is often shorter than the ring finger. Breedlove and colleagues found that finger length patterns for lesbians were more similar to those of men than to those of heterosexual women, and they suggested that as with the ear clicks study, at least some lesbians might have been exposed to higher levels of prenatal androgens than straight women. Neither the ear study nor the finger length study showed a significant difference between gay and straight men.

There was a clear difference, however, between gay and straight men in a recent study that looked at brain responses to odors.[30] Odors from compounds that might be human pheromones were presented to heterosexual women, heterosexual men, and homosexual men. Using brain imaging techniques, researchers found that gay men – like straight women – reacted to the smell of a testosterone derivative. Straight men, by contrast, did not have the same reaction. The researchers concluded that their findings "suggest a link between sexual orientation and hypothalamic neuronal processes."[31]

🕊 ◉ ◉ ◉ 🕊

Is the sexual orientation of adults set by the time they are born? Maybe. The studies described here, taken as a whole, do suggest that there might be a biological basis for sexual orientation. But what does that mean really? In some sense, all behavior can be said to have a biological basis. More specifically, these studies of the biology of sexual orientation show that there are, in some cases, objectively measurable or observable physical traits that differ between straight and gay people. At least some lesbians and gay men seem to have some physical traits that are different from at least some heterosexual people. The implication in the scientific studies described above is that lesbians and gay men (and straight and bisexual people as well) are born that way. At least some homosexual people and heterosexual people are distinct – in some details that have potential biological significance.

Even assuming that these differences are real – a fairly big assumption at this time – what do these biological differences mean? Do these biological differences *cause* people to have a particular sexual orientation? Are some of these biological differences somehow the *effect* of an individual's sexual orientation? Do these differences themselves reflect other underlying factors that somehow cause a particular sexual orientation?

While these questions cannot yet be answered, they tend to provoke interesting discussion, which contributes, in no small part, to the likelihood that a biological study on the topic of sexual orientation will receive media attention that is disproportionate to the amount of coverage that ensues when the average scientific paper is published. As Dean Hamer said about his gay gene research, "there's intense public interest. I was *not* deluged by calls when we discovered the regulator of the metallothionein gene."[32] The studies described here are intriguing, and even if nothing has been proven by them, that makes them newsworthy.

Extensive media coverage of scientific studies on sexual orientation seems to be a reflection of the interests of the general public, both straight and gay. But stories on the science of sexuality tend to be presented by the media rather uncritically. While there is usually another scientist quoted who is skeptical about the research – that makes the story balanced – reporters, perhaps not surprisingly, cannot usually place the research in an appropriate context in the confines of a brief newspaper or magazine article. "Balanced" media coverage also sometimes requires a quote from a right-wing religious person who says that homosexuality is still a sickness no matter what, because the Bible says so. (Though presumably a biological basis for homosexuality does make homophobia a more dicey prospect in that God must have decided to make some people gay.)

The general public and the media in tandem make more of studies on the biological basis of homosexuality than is warranted. They probably make more out of them than some of the scientists involved would like. But beyond that, in recent years the idea has been set in many people's minds that there are biological differences between straight people and gay people and that all of us were probably born with the sexual orientation we have as adults. So even though Dean Hamer's study of the genetics of homosexuality has not been replicated by another lab (the hallmark of proof in the science world), his work has permeated the zeitgeist – the homosexual horse is out of the media barn. People believe in a gay gene. When Hamer's study was published, "gay gene found" was big news. When another team of researchers failed to replicate the original research, "gay gene not found" barely registered in the media.

Because of the work of Dean Hamer, Simon LeVay and others, much of the American general public has grabbed on to the idea that homosexuality is genetic. A biological basis for homosexuality also fits in well with what a lot of gay people feel about themselves. For example, in surveys conducted by *The Advocate*, a national gay newsmagazine, gay men and lesbians were asked about what was at the root of their sexual orientation. Gay men were quite clear: nine out of ten believed that they were born with their sexual orientation, and although "one in five of those men also believes that early childhood environment somehow had something to do with his being gay," only 4% of the respondents thought choice was a factor in their sexual orientation.[33] The responses by lesbians to similar questions were more equivocal, but even so more than half of the women surveyed believed they were born with their sexual orientation, and only 16% believed that choice had any influence on their sexual orientation.[34] (One wonders if straight people are ever asked similar questions.)

As noted at the beginning of this chapter, many people seem to *want* to believe that there are biological differences between people that somehow determine their sexual orientation. This is true both for the general public, as well as at least some of the researchers involved in this type of work. A set and unchanging sexual orientation seems comforting to people. I am what I am and I would have been this way even under dramatically different circumstances. Some people also want to believe in a biologically determined sexual orientation for political reasons: it would be wrong to discriminate against people on the basis of sexual orientation if your sexual orientation is something innate. Indeed, studies show that people are more likely to be supportive of gay and lesbian rights if they believe that homosexuality is something that you are born with and that cannot be changed.[35]

Have political considerations inspired some of the scientists whose work has been described here? Perhaps. At the least, some of the scientists seem very strongly to believe that sexual orientation in general, and homosexual orientation in particular, is something that people were born with. Simon LeVay, for example, believes that the scientific evidence on the nature/nurture question "points to a strong influence of nature, and only a modest influence of nurture."[36] Similarly, J. Michael Bailey concluded after his lesbian sibling study that female sexual orientation is "substantially if not completely innate," and therefore more similar to the case among men than had been supposed.[37] Bailey has also said that "no one has ever found a postnatal social environmental influence for homosexual orientation – and they have looked plenty."[38]

Bailey's studies have tended to include fairly large numbers of people, but that of Simon LeVay and the original study by Dean Hamer were based on the brains of 19 gay men and the DNA of 40 pairs of gay brothers respectively. While it certainly might be the case that LeVay and Hamer have drawn correct conclusions from their studies, it is much too early to state unequivocally that gay people are biologically different from straight people; it is much too early to conclude that lesbians and gay men were born that way. While the research is intriguing, it is essential to keep in mind that even if scientists studying sexual orientation are moving along the right track, the things they are finding do not get at the question of causality. Even if correlation is shown, causality is another giant step beyond that. Perhaps the Xq28 region of the chromosomes of gay men somehow produces a hypothalamus that results in its owner preferring to have sex with men. It is not inconceivable, but it has not been shown – despite what the media might imply in coverage of studies on the biology of homosexuality, and despite what the general public might think.

There do appear to be some measurable, objective (insofar as anything can be said to be objective in a postmodern world) physical differences between straight people and gay people. But keep in mind that these differences are often *average* differences, not categorical. So, for example, some of Simon LeVay's gay brains did not have a "gay" hypothalamus; some of Dean Hamer's pairs of gay brothers did not share the same Xq28 region of their DNA; sometimes – about half the time actually – identical twins are *not* both gay. Is there a single gene for homosexuality in humans? Probably not. Is homosexuality influenced by genes? Quite possibly.

Studies on the biology of homosexuality have been critiqued by scientists for a variety of reasons. These studies have also been criticized from a conceptual standpoint: they are looking at sexuality in a specific time and place and drawing conclusions that seem to apply to humans in general, without regard for cultural or historical considerations. Homosexuality in most scientific studies seems to be treated as a distinct and well-defined category. While bisexuality does exist, in surveys sexual orientation is generally a dichotomous thing: you are either straight or gay. (Bisexuality is sometimes dealt with by including it in the "gay" category: you are either straight or "not straight.") But many people experience sexual behavior as something that evolves and changes over time and depends on their specific circumstances. And many other cultures have entirely different ways of approaching sexuality. The scientific studies described in this chapter view homosexuality through the prism of late twentieth/early twenty-first century Western views of sexuality that often seem to insist that people declare either that they are straight or gay.

A broader perspective is necessary if we are looking at the evolution of homosexuality as a feature of the human species, rather than as a feature of the small subset of humanity that we see around us in America at the beginning of the twenty-first century. How has same-sex eroticism been expressed in other cultures and at other times? Are there cultures in which same-sex eroticism has not been expressed at all? These topics will be explored in Chapters Six and Seven.

CHAPTER SIX

Queer Neighbors

The alphabet of my DNA shapes certain words, but the story is not told. I have to tell it myself.... I can change the story. I am the story.

JEANETTE WINTERSON, THE POWER BOOK[1]

Are people entirely unpredictable or all too predictable? It depends on the day of the week.

Sociobiology recognizes human diversity but tends, for theoretical reasons, to emphasize the things that people have in common. A sociobiological perspective is more likely to emphasize human nature and human universals, whereas anthropologists are more likely to emphasize the extent to which individuals differ because of the influence of the cultures in which they live. From this latter perspective, humans are remarkably diverse, reflecting and in turn affecting the diversity of the world's cultures. The overall perspective of this book is sociobiological, but I do have a healthy regard for the influence of culture on behavior. Within my lifetime for example, American culture has changed for the better in terms of the goals of the women's movement and the civil rights movement. Many people now have opportunities in American society that were not available to them simply because of their sex or race before the 1960s. Racism and sexism continue to be problems, but it does seem as if many of the "facts" that people took for granted when I was a child have now been entirely discredited.

As a general rule, people, the things people do, and the motivations behind those actions are complicated. It is difficult to imagine that a person can ever really be referred to as "simple"; it is utterly inconceivable that a group of people might be described that way. Groups of people are exponentially more complex than the individuals of which they are composed. Groups of people create something that is larger than the sum of their parts; they create cultures. Cultures are an emergent property of human groups, that is, cultures have something of a life of their own, beyond the simple adding together of the lives of the individuals involved.

Cultures are the intellectual province of cultural anthropology, the field which studies "mankind." Mankind was meant rather literally throughout most of the field's history in that men were generally studying other men. More recent decades though have seen a greater emphasis on women and their influence in cultures throughout the world. Anthropology as an academic discipline traditionally includes four sub-fields: sociocultural anthropology, biological anthropology, anthropological linguistics and archeology. Although each of these specialties is integral to the "study of man," when people are talking about anthropology, they are usually talking about sociocultural anthropology and that field is the subject of this chapter and the next.

Anthropology is, in some ways, more of an approach to a topic than a particular topic in itself. For example, detailed accounts by travelers from hundreds of years ago about the people they encountered and their ways of life could, in retrospect, be thought of as anthropology, despite the fact that the field could not really be said to exist as a distinct specialization at the time these accounts were written. The hallmark of sociocultural anthropology is participant-observation. A person who is studying a culture participates in it by living in it for some period of time. The result of this experience often becomes a book called an ethnography, or description of a way of life. While this method of study ties sociocultural anthropology together, the specific topics any given anthropologist might examine are diverse. Perennial favorites include kinship, religion, rituals, economics, and politics. More recently, gender has become an important focus in anthropology.

Anthropologists traditionally have studied smaller-scale "primitive" societies but the approach is one that can be used anywhere there are people who live in groups or who form subgroups within larger entities that are distinct in some way. So, for example, it is conceivable that an anthropologist could spend some time going to professional baseball games and then write an ethnography of Boston Red Sox fans. The method of study – participant-observation – would make this an anthropological work.

Sociocultural anthropology has changed a great deal since the nineteenth century when white men started leaving their comfortable European armchairs to explore in person the lives of the "savages" and "primitives," who usually lived far from the centers of Euro-American civilization. Early anthropologists were often on salvage missions, recognizing that the world was changing rapidly and traditional ways of life were in danger of disappearing. Early on, anthropologists thought and wrote about "Weltanschauung" or worldview, and tried to convey the idea of cultural relativism. Western Europeans and Americans have particular ways of looking at things, and people in other cultures also have their own particular ways of looking at things. The differences between groups make sense if you consider the perspective and logic of the "other." (Although cultural relativism is somewhat archaic in anthropology, it remains a concept that more Americans – perhaps more people in general – might find useful.)

By the end of the twentieth century, postmodernism had taken hold in the field of cultural anthropology. The old authorities were questioned, especially since the authority was frequently a privileged white man telling other people like himself about the lives of people from countries that the white men had colonized. To postmodernists, the early anthropologists were essentially more intellectually oriented imperialists. Since there is no single American or British viewpoint, for example, it follows logically that there is no single, unitary Japanese perspective or Javanese perspective. To pretend otherwise is to deny the importance of individuals and the power relationships that spring up in any social group – not to mention power disparities between groups. Some people make decisions that have a great impact on other people's lives and it is impossible to even think that an entire culture can be summarized. In postmodernism, facts themselves are questioned and considered to be a matter of perspective. Monolithic Weltanschauung, R.I.P.

Postmodernism is in some ways a very important idea: individual people do, after all, play multiple roles in societies and have varying perspectives that are dependent upon their place(s) within a group or within a hierarchy. Furthermore, cultures themselves change over time: cultures have histories and they interact with other cultures and with entities created indigenously and those that are imported from (or imposed by) other cultures. Early anthropology was often written in a timeless present as if the lives of the "primitives" were static and only Euro-American cultures had histories.[2]

While the postmodernist perspective is valuable in some ways, the problem is that this view threatens, ultimately, to reduce cultural anthropology to irrelevance. If there isn't a Javanese perspective or a Japanese perspective, what then can cultural anthropology tell us? That every individual human has her or his own unique view of the world? That seems fairly obvious. Between political correctness and postmodernism, cultural anthropology is currently in danger of being deconstructed right out of existence. It is a field of inquiry that has surprisingly little influence in our culture, even as Americans continue to grapple with the ramifications of multiculturalism, immigration, the politics of inclusion, and the role of America in the world.

Any summaries of human behavior will have their limitations. You can try to say what it feels like to be Japanese or Javanese, you can summarize, talk about averages and what is typically seen, but there will pretty much always be exceptions to any rules about human behavior, either on an individual level ("I do know one person who doesn't like chocolate") or at the level of cultures ("Among the ABC people exactly the opposite situation exists ..."). As Dostoyevsky might have pointed out, it is almost impossible to predict what an individual person will do or why he will do it. Similarly, as someone said of the character played by Humphrey Bogart in the movie *Casablanca*, "He's a difficult customer, that Rick. One never knows what he'll do or why."

With the disclaimer that summaries are inherently limiting, I am going to try to summarize the existence of homosexuality among humans in different cultures in this chapter and the next. Anthropologists tend not to write summaries like this as often as you might think they would. Why is this the case? Cultural anthropology generally celebrates diversity and summaries take some of the fun out of diversity. It is, after all, rather presumptuous to interpret the meanings of other people's lives and latter day cultural anthropologists generally try to be aware of racism and their highly privileged role in the world. In fact, a fair bit of anthropology at this point in time tends to focus on what it means to be an anthropologist and what it means to "do" anthropology. This "reflexive anthropology" would probably look askance at much of the following.

Cultural anthropology probably has an undeserved reputation as a field that has boldly explored human sexuality.[3] A few very influential anthropologists in the early part of the twentieth century wrote a few very influential books on the topic of sex, but for the most part the field has said remarkably little on the topic of human sexuality, even as anthropologists have spilled enough ink to fill oil tankers on the subjects of marriage and kinship – aspects of human life that presumably are at least related to sex. For every Margaret Mead or Bronislaw Malinowski who wrote about human sexuality, there were dozens of anthropologists who barely mentioned that sex was a part of the lives of the people they studied. In part this is because anthropologists are generally describing cultures rather than the specific behaviors from which cultures ultimately derive. But this reticence on the topic of sexuality was also a reflection of anthropology's roots in Victorian culture – early anthropologists were often as sexually repressed as others of their cultural background and social class were. Given this context, you can imagine that information on the topic of homosexuality in other cultures is frequently lacking.

For example, Bronislaw Malinowski, one of cultural anthropology's founding fathers, published the interestingly titled *The Sexual Life of Savages* in 1929.[4] That volume was an "ethnographic account of courtship, marriage and family life among the natives of the Trobriand Islands, British New Guinea." Homosexuality is mentioned a few times in this 600-page book. Malinowski tells us that "homosexual intercourse, bestiality, exhibitionism, oral and anal eroticism … are … regarded by the natives as inadequate and contemptible substitutes for the proper exercise of the sexual impulse."[5] The few other details about same-sex sexuality among the Trobrianders are actually, I think, less interesting than the index to *The Sexual Life of Savages* which lists the pages that you can refer to if you want to see what Malinowski – I mean the Trobrianders – had to say about "Homosexuality: contempt for and repugnance to" and "Homosexuality: unnatural conditions conducive to."[6]

Did Malinowski himself – like so many of his Western contemporaries – find homosexuality to be repugnant? Did he believe that "unnatural conditions" were conducive to homosexuality?[7] In short, did Malinowski find exactly what a privileged white male European born in the nineteenth century might expect to find out about homosexuality when he lived among the Trobrianders? Perhaps many anthropologists left Euro-American cultures in the earlier part of the twentieth century to live among the "natives" and found what they themselves already knew from their own cultures – that homosexuality is repugnant. One anthropologist who, to give him some credit, did at least want to discuss the topic asked his informants if they "had ever been subjected to an unnatural practice."[8]

It seems conceivable that some Euro-American anthropologists failed to see homosexuality among their subjects because they themselves were unaware that same-sex eroticism existed in their own culture, or could even exist, period. Perhaps yet other anthropologists who knew that some people in their own culture were *that way* were relieved not to see evidence of same-sex eroticism during their fieldwork ("Thank God I don't even have to mention it because it isn't there!"). Perhaps some anthropologists arrived to study the "savages" at some point after Christian missionaries had arrived at the same locale. The "savages" in this case might have already caught on that merely mentioning the existence of same-sex eroticism to the Westerners was a bad idea.

It certainly seems possible that the preconceived notions and prejudices of anthropologists working among the "primitives" are at the root of the fact that there has long been a dearth of some very basic information on the topic of homosexuality in other cultures. It is also logically possible however that in fact homosexuality as it is currently conceived in the West is in fact unknown among many of the world's cultures. What has anthropology in general had to say on this topic?

Some twentieth century American anthropologists, including Margaret Mead, believed that some people in all cultures are sexually oriented toward others of the same sex.[9] Whether or not this orientation was something that could be expressed in any given culture, and the appropriate ways in which it would be expressed, vary from one culture to another. The idea that all cultures include people who might be, in our culture, described as homosexual is something that no one can prove. Nor can anyone disprove that idea. But this idea would probably be repudiated by many cultural anthropologists today because sexuality is thought to be "socially constructed" – it is conceptualized differently in different places (more on this topic shortly). Even though it is contentious, the idea that some people in any given culture are homosexually oriented regardless of whether or not homosexuality is expressed will be the perspective that I adopt for discussion's sake when we turn to the topic of the evolution of homosexuality in Chapter Eight.

In retrospect, latter day anthropologists have recognized the shortcomings of their field regarding the study of homosexuality. According to Kath Weston, "throughout the first half of the [twentieth] century, most allusions by anthropologists to homosexual behavior remained as veiled in ambiguity and as couched in judgment as were references to homosexuality in the dominant discourse of the surrounding society."[10] According to Thomas Fitzgerald, anthropological writings "dealing with the subject of homosexuality have suffered from being excessively cryptic and generally nonanalytical."[11] Ethnographies may have had subtext, but the texts themselves were usually lacking specific information on same-sex sexual behavior. By the 1960s and 1970s, however, this began to change. As homosexuality became more of an openly discussed topic in general in American culture, anthropology also began to look at it as a subject that had been unfairly neglected by researchers.

In 1966, David Sonenschein noted that "anthropologists have ignored homosexuality in Western societies and, what is worse, have barely taken note of it as it manifests itself in primitive groups."[12] Sonenschein's "plea for research" was followed fairly quickly by resolutions of the American Anthropological Association in 1970 that sought to legitimize research on homosexuality.[13] Influential anthropologist E.E. Evans-Pritchard of Oxford University published a paper on "Sexual inversion among the Azande," also in 1970.[14] Interestingly,

Evans-Pritchard's publication of this paper had been deliberately delayed.[15] The fieldwork upon which it was based took place 40 years before the paper was finally published.[16]

Also around this time a paper was published by English sociologist Mary McIntosh that was to become very influential in the anthropology of homosexuality.[17] While the paper itself is interesting and relatively straightforward, it ultimately makes discussions of homosexuality in non-Western cultures far more complex. The gist of McIntosh's argument is that homosexuality is a social role that "does not exist in all societies, and where it does it is not always the same as in modern western societies."[18] In some societies "there may be much homosexual behavior, but there are no 'homosexuals.'"[19] This is an important point. It is akin to the suggestion in Chapter Four that although there is much homosexual behavior seen in nonhuman primates, no monkeys or apes could be considered to be "homosexual." A distinction here is being made between a *category* (individuals who are homosexually oriented) and a *description* (behavior that is homosexual, in that the parties involved are both of the same biological sex).

McIntosh's ideas became melded to those of the very influential French social theorist Michel Foucault in an approach to behavior known as "social constructionism." Social constructionists would argue that "sexual orientation cannot be properly or completely understood apart from the social milieu in which it is embedded."[20] Further, "constructionists view sexuality as the result of complex, diffuse experiences. Partner preferences result from idiosyncratic personality requirements, socially structured opportunities, and cultural norms."[21]

Foucault wrote that "the nineteenth century and [twentieth] have been ... the age of multiplication: a dispersion of sexualities, a strengthening of their disparate forms, a multiple implantation of 'perversions.' Our epoch has initiated sexual heterogeneities."[22] (It should be noted that despite Foucault's assertion, it seems quite possible that the "perversions" always existed and the change wrought by the past hundred years or so is that the topic of perversity is now open for discussion.) Homosexuality was first given a name in the Western medical literature in the nineteenth century, and according to Foucault, "the homosexual was now a species."[23] While I would agree that naming something often confers legitimacy on it – and even to a certain extent can make things real – the social constructionist school of thought, of which Foucault was a founding father, takes his ideas as well as those of McIntosh and elaborates them to what sometimes seem to be an absurd level. Yes, of course, the expression of sexuality is influenced by culture. But some of the true devotees of social constructionism go so far as to argue that homosexuality did not exist before it was named in the Western European world in 1869.[24] Some would argue that "by creating categories within the sphere of sexual relations science does more than give a simple description of a reality – it invents sexual categories and claims them to be universal."[25]

The academic alternative to social constructionism is known as essentialism and in its extreme form it is as misguided as its antithesis. "In the social sciences today, and specifically in sexology, essentialism ... implies a belief that certain phenomena are natural, inevitable, universal, and biologically determined."[26] Essentialists, essentially, would argue that gay people have always existed and can be found in all of the world's cultures.[27] People who believe that homosexuality is biologically based are more likely to be found in this camp than among the social constructionists.

Both these groups of academics seem to be ignoring some important points made by their rivals. Similarly both groups seem to have some problems with terminology. Namely, the difference between homosexuality *as a category* (that is opposed to the category of heterosexuality), and a more basic same-sex erotic *desire*.[28] The latter can exist without the former. The anthropological evidence seems to indicate that there are cultures in which homosexuality is unknown as a concept. That does not however suggest, let alone prove, that those societies are devoid of individuals who might *desire* sexual contact with others of the same biological sex. Are there gay people as defined in the West in every culture? No, apparently not. Do some people in every culture experience homosexual desire? No one knows the answer to that question; it might or might not be the case. If there is a gay gene, it could well be the case that some people in every culture experience desire for their own sex.

While Foucault and many of his intellectual descendents are far too vague for my tastes, it is almost certainly true that in some ways homosexuality, and sexuality more generally, can be said to be constructed. Anthropologist Carole Vance has written lucidly on the topic of the construction of sexuality and her "invaluable commentaries … are among the most cogent available in any discipline."[29] "At minimum," Vance writes,

> "all social construction approaches adopt the view that physically identical sexual acts may have varying social significance and subjective meaning depending on how they are defined and understood in different cultures and historical periods."[30]

So far, so good. But then some people working in this paradigm go further and suggest that whether an individual is erotically attracted to men, women, or both is also something that is constructed:

> "… object choice (heterosexuality, homosexuality and bisexuality, as contemporary sexology would conceptualize it) is not intrinsic or inherent in the individual, but is constructed from more polymorphous possibilities."[31]

Perhaps. In what Vance then refers to as the most radical form of constructionist theory, adherents to this version of the paradigm question the existence of any inherent sexuality *in the human body*, and

> "entertain the idea that there is no essential, undifferentiated sexual 'impulse,' 'sex drive,' or 'lust,' which resides in the body due to physiological functioning and sensation. Sexual desire, then, is itself constructed by culture and history from the energies and capacities of the body."[32]

Sexual desires "are no longer assumed to be intrinsic or perhaps even necessary."[33]

Ok, now perhaps we have gone a bit too far. It seems to me that an excellent case can be made for the social constructionist minimum described above. Sex means different things to different people, even within one culture. Little imagination is needed to extrapolate from that point to other places and other times. Indeed anyone who has ever taken an anthropology course or anyone who can conceptualize beyond their own specific circumstances probably would not argue the point that sexuality is at least somewhat subjective. But what about object choice? What about whether a person is erotically attracted to their own sex, the opposite sex or both? Is this something that is constructed, or is it something that is a deeply felt and perhaps unalterable facet of an individual's personality? That is the proverbial $64,000 question. Evidence – good evidence – could probably be found that would support both the idea that sexual orientation is constructed as well as the idea that an individual's particular sexual object choice is something that is inherent. For example, on the constructionist side of the debate, the effects of homophobia on an individual's "true" sexual orientation should not be underestimated. Being raised in a culture that despises gay people is very likely to have an impact on an individual's object choice. Whether or not there is an innate sexual preference in humans is not likely to be an objectively answerable question, much like questions that ask if it is nature or nurture are not likely to be definitively answerable.

The form of the social constructionist paradigm that Vance describes as the most radical considers sexual desire in general to be problematic. Can sexuality exist without cultural influence? Probably not. There probably isn't a "pure" human sexuality that is uninfluenced by cultures. But does sexuality reside somewhere within the body human? This is a point at which I would definitely part company with the radical constructionists. Humans are apes and like the other apes, humans have sex. People are not different from their fellow apes in this regard. This continuity of behavior between these taxonomic groups certainly seems to me to imply that sexuality is not entirely constructed. A sexual impulse exists in apes *and* humans. Evolution would not have it any other way. Contrary to the radical social constructionists, sexual desire is "necessary."

One of the strengths of the social constructionist school is that its practitioners try to step outside conventional wisdom and look at things from a unique perspective. They consider the assumptions that many other people make implicitly. Unfortunately, this stepping outside can also take people too far away from one of the most important lessons we can take from sociobiology: humans are animals that have evolved over millions of years. The aspects of human life that can be said to be "intrinsic" are probably common to the apes and to many other animals.

Given that the social constructionist school has been the dominant paradigm in cultural anthropology for some years, reading the anthropological literature on homosexuality can make you question whether you even know the meaning of the word homosexuality. This is probably not a bad thing on the whole, even though it does make things rather complicated if you are trying to write a cross-cultural summary of homosexuality. With the foregoing discussion of social constructionism as a substantial caveat, what have anthropologists had to say about the presence and absence of homosexual people in non-Western cultures?[34] What have anthropologists had to say about forms of sexuality that seem akin to what many in the West think of as homosexuality?

In the early 1950s, around the time the Kinsey reports were being published, Clellan Ford and Frank Beach published *Patterns of Sexual Behavior*,[35] in which they considered a variety of topics related to human sexuality from both a cross-cultural and cross-species perspective. Of the 76 societies for which they had information, Ford and Beach found that 49 groups or 64% considered "homosexual activities of one sort or another [to be] normal and socially acceptable for certain members of the community."[36] In the remaining groups, "homosexual activities on the part of adults are reported to be totally absent, rare, or carried on only in secrecy."[37] Ford and Beach note that in the latter groups, homosexuality is generally condemned and thus is likely to be more common than people let on. After considering homosexual behavior in other species, Ford and Beach concluded that even though homosexual behavior is never the most common type of sexual activity in adults of any society or any species, it represents the expression of "a biological tendency" in most mammals, including humans.[38]

For most of the rest of the twentieth century, cross-cultural summaries of homosexuality were relatively rare. One anthropologist noted that in the more than 40 years that elapsed between Ford and Beach's publication and his paper on the same topic in 1995, "the cross-cultural database on homosexuality has grown only marginally and is still dramatically flawed in ways that make it difficult to investigate all but the simplest of hypotheses."[39] Rather than comparative, cross-cultural studies, the trend in the latter half of the twentieth century was for anthropologists to write in-depth accounts of specific cultural practices rather than broad summaries that considered a variety of social groups.[40]

More recently though there have been a few books that have attempted to summarize the ways in which same-sex desire is expressed in the world's diverse cultures. In 1997, influential anthropologist Gilbert Herdt published *Same Sex, Different Cultures: Gays and Lesbians Across Cultures*.[41] Herdt's entire discussion of this topic makes for worthwhile reading. Points he makes that are relevant here include: (1) "one of the great problems of sexual study, particularly of homosexuality, is how many cultures simply lack categories or general concepts that cover the meanings of the contemporary notion of homosexual"[42]; (2) nevertheless, "it is likely that not only [same-gender] desire but also the practice of same-gender sexual relations in one form or another occur in all or nearly all human societies"[43]; (3) that does not imply however that what Westerners think of as homosexuality is universal among humans: "rather than asking whether homosexuality is universal, then, we might be wiser to ask if same-gender relations occur in all times and places, what the optimal conditions are for the expression of same-sex desire, and how cultures and historical periods influence and treat these roles and behaviors when they do occur."[44]

Two other relatively recent volumes also explore same-sex eroticism in non-Western cultures. The first of these is *Female Desires: Same-Sex Relations and Transgender Practices Across Cultures*, a volume edited by Evelyn Blackwood and S.E. Wieringa and published in 1999.[45] Despite the editors' adherence to the concepts espoused by the social constructionist school, this volume includes important information on female-female sexual practices that are often either ignored or dismissed in the work of other – frequently male – anthropologists. Also fairly recently published was *Homosexualities* by Stephen O. Murray[46] which exhaustively reviews cross-cultural work on same-sex sexual practices, and brings together Murray's own extensive research and publications.

Homosexualities is organized around a scheme that considers homosexual behaviors in non-Western cultures to be classifiable into one of three categories.[47] Variations on such classification systems have been around since the 1960s[48] and help make sense of a rather large array of cultural practices. Same-sex erotic relations are often categorized as transgenerational (if the individuals involved are from different age groups), transgendered (if the individuals involved adopt some of the cultural practices that are usually adopted by people of the opposite biological sex in their culture) or egalitarian (the individuals involved have roughly equivalent status within the social group). Modern Western homosexuality is generally classified as egalitarian in these classification systems; examples of transgenerational and transgendered same-sex relations will be discussed in some depth in Chapter Seven. These classification systems while often claiming to be applicable to both female and male same-sex eroticism are generally based on information about male sexual practices, and "data on female sexuality rarely enter into the analysis."[49]

🦅 ◉ ◉ ◉ 🦅

Arguments about the existence of and the extent of homosexuality in non-Western cultures run the gamut from those that echo the popular gay liberation slogan from some years back that "We are everywhere" to others that suggest that homosexuality as Westerners know it is something that simply is not found in all societies. Are there in fact societies in which homosexuality as a concept is entirely unknown? It seems as if this is a possibility. At the very least there do seem to be societies in which no one is publicly known to be having sexual relationships with other individuals of the same biological sex.

The question remains, however, whether there are individuals who are erotically attracted to their own sex but for whom there is no possibility to act on these desires.

Social scientists seem to be in agreement: (1) "the cross-cultural evidence suggests that life-long or exclusive homosexuality is a rare phenomenon"[50]; (2) "cases of *exclusive* homosexuality appear to be relatively rare"[51]; and (3) "exclusive homosexuality ... because of the cultural dictums concerning marriage and the family, appears to be generally excluded as a sexual option even in those societies where homosexual behavior is generally approved."[52] The summary point bears repeating: homosexuality, as it is known in the West, apparently is not known in all societies and when it is known, exclusive or lifelong homosexuality is quite rare in terms of the numbers of individuals involved.

During most of the lifespan of the human species, our ancestors made a living by hunting and gathering food. It has only been relatively recently that agriculture has been used to provide most or all of the foods that many humans rely upon. Humans evolved in this context of foraging for, rather than growing, food. From an evolutionary perspective, the presence or absence of homosexuality in hunter-gatherer groups is significant: while groups of humans who hunt and gather today or who recently lived this way certainly are not the equivalent of human ancestors, foragers can give anthropologists hints about how our forebears might have lived. It is interesting – and probably significant from the perspective of the evolution of homosexuality – that homosexuality is less common in forager societies than in agricultural societies.[53]

Why is there little homosexuality among today's hunter-gatherers? Social constructionists would probably say that homosexuality was not a part of the array of cultural possibilities in many hunter-gatherer societies. But although that may well be the case, it begs the question: even if a culture does not recognize a category of or type of person who is sexually oriented towards others of the same biological sex, it does not necessarily follow logically that no "gay people" exist in that culture. Saying that there is "no homosexuality" in a given culture means that no category of "homosexual person" exists and/or there are no people who are solely and presumably publicly identified as such. That does not say anything about behavior though, and it certainly does not come close to saying anything about desire. There could easily be same-sex behavior going on or, absent the behavior, there may nonetheless be a desire for such behavior – even if it is not expressed or acted upon – on the part of some people.

Even without homosexuality as a category – even without "the homosexual" as a "species" to use Foucault's term – might homosexual desire exist in all cultures among at least some individuals? It seems possible that this is the case, although it certainly cannot be proven. But if there is no category or concept of homosexual person in a given group, individuals are quite unlikely to be identified as such or to identify themselves as such. Especially to some strange anthropologist.

This harkens back to what Margaret Mead and some other early anthropologists believed – that people with homosexual inclinations exist in all societies, but whether this is expressed and how it is expressed varies. For the purposes of discussion of how a gene for homosexuality might have evolved, I will make an assumption in Chapter Eight that homosexual desire on the part of some individuals in every social group is a cultural universal. Before we get to that though we are going to take a closer look at three cultures in which same-sex desire seems to have had a distinct outlet that is different from, and yet resonates with, what Westerners think of as homosexuality.

CHAPTER SEVEN

Three Lives

Paris offered [Gertrude] Stein the privacy and personal freedom to live and write as she pleased .... It was only in France that Stein was able to develop a "personal life" in which she could express her sexuality.

SHARI BENSTOCK, WOMEN OF THE LEFT BANK: PARIS 1900-1940[1]

Was Gertrude Stein the world's first lesbian? It seems rather unlikely, but the American writer who lived in Paris for most of her life might at least have been the world's most famous lesbian up until the 1997 national coming out party for Ellen DeGeneres that took place on American television. Gertrude Stein, self-styled genius, author of impenetrable, repetitious prose, and "husband" to the doting Alice B. Toklas, is significant to the story being told in this book because she was a woman unlike nearly all the innumerable women who lived before her. This was not only because she was publicly known to be a lesbian, but also, perhaps more significantly, Stein had money. It was feasible for Gertrude Stein to make a life for herself that included a female partner with whom she lived outside of the context of marriage to a man. Stein had not been married off in her youth to a suitable male by her parents – a fate which has awaited the vast majority of women since the dawn of man (sic). Stein had the freedom, and the cash, to do what she wanted.

There have been very few places and times in which more than a few women have had the kind of freedom Stein enjoyed. A lack of information on lesbians in Western history and in other cultures may be the result of their stories being repressed, but, logically speaking, it might also be a reflection of the fact that most women who have ever lived were unable to express desire they might have felt for other women because of the practical and/or economic circumstances of their lives.

In the world of the anthropology of homosexuality, quite a bit more is known about same-sex sexual behavior among men than among women. Is this because male sexuality is more visible? More extravagant? More important? Maybe, maybe, and no. But it is definitely the case that less is known about same-sex desire among women. Is this desire less common in women than in men? Perhaps that is the case, or perhaps women's sexuality has been constrained in a variety of ways in many different cultures. Perhaps same-sex desire among women can be expressed only when women have viable options outside life in traditional nuclear-type family units. As a practical matter, women are unlikely to express a clear and exclusive sexual preference for other women if they have to marry men in order to survive. The extent of same-sex desire among women cannot be known until more women have the freedoms that many men (and Gertrude Stein) have enjoyed to participate in a world in which they have their own resources and are able to make more of their own decisions. Stein's contemporary Virginia Woolf knew that a woman needs a room of her own in order to achieve great things; Gertrude knew that a good income and a wife could also be very, very helpful.

Lesbian lives have been nearly invisible to mainstream American culture up until quite recently. This invisibility seems to have been common historically and cross-culturally as well. Are there stories of lesbian lives that have yet to be told? Undoubtedly. But logically it could also be true that anthropologists and historians have not described lesbian subcultures very often because such subcultures simply did not exist. Homosexuality among women may be less common, and therefore less commonly described, than male homosexuality because there have been few times and places in which women were free to be gay. Would more women be lesbians if they could live outside the rules of patriarchy? I am just guessing here, but I am guessing yes.

In 1980, intellectual/poet/lesbian Adrienne Rich published an essay called "Compulsory Heterosexuality and Lesbian Existence"[2] in which she explored heterosexuality as a political institution.[3] Rich was writing, she said, "to challenge the *erasure* of lesbian existence from so much of scholarly feminist literature (emphasis added)."[4] According to Rich, "the fact is that women in every culture and throughout history *have* undertaken the task of independent, nonheterosexual, woman-connected existence, to the extent made possible by their context, often in the belief that they were the 'only ones' ever to have done so."[5] Rich may be right: the stories of lesbian lives may have been actively erased from history. I would suggest, however, that it was not the case that the stories had been *erased*, but rather that the stories – assuming that some women have always been attracted to other women – were rarely allowed to *unfold* because of social and economic constraints on female behavior. Rather than a conspiracy to silence the fact of lesbian existence, I would suggest that the conspiracy, if that is the right word, has been to circumvent lesbian existence as a part of the more general oppression of women that is such an integral part of so many of the world's cultures.

With all due respect to the women of the world, a parallel situation exists among human females and among female monkeys and apes. It was suggested in Chapter Four that in nonhuman primates the possibility that a female might be able to express a clear and exclusive sexual preference for other females is likely to be highly constrained, if not obliterated, by male sexual coercion. From the perspective of male monkeys and apes, females are a resource they use to pass along their genes. Human females have similarly been seen as something of a reproductive resource for males in a wide variety of cultures. In many places and at many times, female sexuality has been constrained and controlled by males. This is true in monkeys, apes, and humans.[6]

Adrienne Rich's essay focuses on individuals and my focus here is really on broader cultural practices. Even though my view is somewhat different from hers, the phrase "compulsory heterosexuality" remains evocative, much as the essay itself continues to be thought provoking, a quarter century after its publication. And it remains true that in the world today many women – and many men as well – continue to face the reality of compulsory heterosexuality.

How common is homosexuality in general among humans? This is not something that can be quantified even in America in the twenty-first century – and we have an entire industry that is devoted to counting and surveying the populace. What about other places and other times? It is really hard to say how common homosexuality is or was. As is the case with nonhuman animals, we can say for sure that heterosexual behavior is far more common than homosexual behavior. But with six billion people, thousands of years of recorded history, and hundreds of cultures, there is plenty of homosexual behavior to write about.

Homosexuality, *as it is known today in the modern West*, seems to have been very uncommon in other places and other times. But there are plenty of other ways of doing things: there is a large variety of ways homosexual desire can be and has been expressed in different cultures. Even in the modern West, homosexual behavior is variable and only some people fit the stereotype that is the basis for the idea upon which this book is based. That stereotype goes something like this: from an early age, some people believe themselves to be "different" from others. This difference often goes unnamed but is at some point retrospectively identified as a sexual orientation or more general attraction towards others of the same biological sex. This orientation/attraction is fairly often repressed in youth. Concurrently, these individuals face a substantial amount of family and/or peer pressure to date and eventually marry someone of the opposite sex. At some point in the lives of these "different" people however, "coming out" occurs, which is an acknowledgment of same-sex desire. Thereafter, the individuals in question live an exclusive life of being attracted to and having sex with people of the same biological sex. The implication being that this finding oneself and the subsequent exclusivity somehow reflects the true nature of these individuals. That is, "I was different from the other kids. I was always gay but for a long time it wasn't something I could express or even name. But now that I've come out, I'm not going back!" (This stereotype might be less valid for younger lesbian and gay Americans who have grown up in a culture in which homosexuality is a widely discussed topic in the American mass media, to the point where a gay character is likely to be found in every television series.)

If someone who feels "different" as a child lives in a society in which homosexuality as a concept or as a way of organizing one's life simply does not exist, then that person cannot, as a practical matter, be "gay," no matter what their desires might be.

This book started off pointing out that homosexuality as it is often experienced in the modern West is an evolutionary conundrum: exclusive same-sex sexual desire should not exist because of natural selection. If gay people have gay genes, these genes should be selected against, and should, logically, die out if their bearers only have sex with others of the same biological sex. But the Western model of homosexuality is pretty unusual. Much more commonly observed throughout history and across cultures is a rather fluid bisexuality in which people who have sex with others of their own biological sex, also have sex with people of the opposite sex, usually in the context of marriage. Is this still a conundrum? Yes, but less of one than a Western perspective implies, in that reproduction is likely to still be occurring.

The Western model is rare in other places and other times, and it certainly is not universal in the West either. Heterosexual marriage by contrast is a cultural universal – all cultures include the idea that males and females should be in some sort of partnership with each other that generally involves sex and offspring.[7] In addition to being a *cultural* universal (the tradition is found in all cultures), it is also essentially an *individual* universal in many traditional societies – *every* individual who reaches an appropriate age is expected to marry someone of the opposite sex. Exceptions are rare. Therefore, across numerous or perhaps most of the world's cultures, homosexual desire, assuming it exists in at least some individuals, would be expressed in a context that also includes heterosexual sex and likely reproduction. This is the case for two of the three traditions that will be discussed at greater length in the rest of this chapter. And this compulsory heterosexuality has ramifications for the evolution of homosexuality that will be discussed further in Chapter Eight.

Many anthropologists have used typologies to categorize the variety of ways that homosexual desire has been expressed in different cultures. Homosexual relationships are often described as transgenerational, transgendered, or egalitarian. Modern Western homosexuality is generally considered to be egalitarian in that relationships often, though of course not always, occur between individuals who are of roughly the same age and social status. Transgenerational homosexual relations occur when the individuals in question are from different age groups – the ancient Greeks (older men with a fondness for handsome boys), and the Sambians of Melanesia (teenage boys from different age grades having sex with each other) will be discussed further shortly. The transgenerational variety of homosexual life is more common in other cultures than you might think, given how disturbed many people in

America are about the topic of large age differences in sexual partners (unless, of course, we are talking about heterosexuals like Jack Nicholson and Donald Trump and their starlets du jour). In transgendered homosexual relations, one member of any homosexual dyad is considered to be something other than a run-of-the-mill man or women – they are thought in some cases to be a member of a third gender. The third gendered person sometimes winds up having sex with someone of a more traditional gender – who also happens to be the same biological sex that they are.

The next few pages describe variability in homosexual behavior in three different cultural traditions. These are rather well known examples of what modern Westerners might think of as "homosexual cultures," or three cultures that resonate with what Westerners think of as homosexuality, even though they are substantially different from the recent Western model.

Ancient Greece. There has been something of a cover-up. The culture of ancient Greece, widely considered to be at the root of Western civilization, turns out to be a place where males were having a lot of sex with other males. As if this is not shocking enough, the sex in question was particularly prevalent in two contexts: within the military, and between older men and boys.

Who knew? Actually many people do know this, despite the fact that speaking about same-sex sexuality was not encouraged in polite Western society for a very long time. The cover-up of this ghastly information ultimately failed, and now many people know that the civilization that begat our own (via the Roman Empire and Europe) was full of the kind of people that give Antonin Scalia conniptions.

Homoeroticism was a celebrated aspect of the lives of many men in ancient Greece, especially those from the ruling classes. This is generally considered to be an example of age-structured or transgenerational homosexuality in that the individuals involved were often, though not always, from different age groups. Older men fairly often had younger male lovers, in addition to having wives. "The structural relationship between the older and the younger male in ancient Greece was formalized by a code of honor and love ... [but] for the Greeks, these customs did not oppose marriage or fatherhood. Indeed, a Greek citizen could not achieve full personhood unless he married into the proper family and fathered children to carry on the family name and estate ...."[8] Many or perhaps most ruling class men in ancient Greece were married to women and had something of a nuclear family life, even though much of their time and energy was devoted to exploring and expressing their sexual interests in other men, or boys to be more specific.

This pattern was the predominant one among the ruling class males in ancient Athens, which was the most culturally advanced of the ancient Greek city-states. In Sparta, which was the most militaristic of the city-states, homosexual relationships between male citizens seem to have been universal.[9] As among the Athenians, Spartan males were expected also to be married to women, with whom they would have children. In the words of Stephen O. Murray,[10] in Sparta, "when it came time to marry and to sire children ... males continued to sleep, as usual, with their male age mates, slipping into their wives' bedchamber only long enough to perform their conjugal duty in the dark." Among the Spartans, "exclusive pederasty was negatively sanctioned, but pederasty was expected."[11] In ancient Thebes, the "Sacred Band" was a group of 150 pairs of male warrior/lovers who fought together. It was thought by some that organizing an army on the basis of couples was a more effective way of preparing for battle than organizing the warriors on the basis of biological kinship, because "a band cemented by friendship grounded upon love is never broken, and is invincible."[12] So much for don't ask, don't tell.

Interestingly, the ancient Greeks had no words that correspond with our relatively recent terms for the concept of homosexuality or a homosexual person.[13] "With few exceptions, the Greeks assumed that ordinarily sexual choices were not mutually exclusive, but rather that people were generally capable of responding erotically to beauty in both sexes. Often they could and did."[14] In our terms, it was expected in ancient Greece that people (which usually meant men in that particularly patriarchal time) had the capacity for bisexuality. Nevertheless, "it was recognized that some men preferred women, and others, male partners."[15]

The Symposium by Plato contains what may be the first explanation for human sexual diversity ever written. In *The Symposium*, when it is the turn of the playwright Aristophanes to get up and speak to the others about love, he explains that long ago, people were double the size they are today – these ancestral humans were essentially two people melded together back to back. Some of the pairs were made up of a female half and a male half, some were made up of two female halves, and some were made up of two male halves. The gods decided that these pairs must be split – and so they were, and ever since that time, people are destined to spend their lives searching for their "missing half." Individuals who were originally part of an opposite-sex pair search for an opposite-sex person, and individuals who were originally part of a same-sex pair are looking for an "other half" of the same sex.[16] In this particular creation story, homosexual males who marry women and have children do so "under the compulsion of custom, without natural inclination."[17]

The Sambia. Melanesia is a group of islands in the southwestern Pacific that has always been very popular with anthropologists. Included within that group is the big island of Papua New Guinea/Irian Jaya. One of the particularly interesting aspects of life in this culture area is that a fairly substantial number of Melanesian societies – perhaps 10-20%[18] – have rituals that were inspired by a rather unusual cultural concept. That concept is that young boys need the help of older boys and men in order to grow strong and develop into adults. More specifically, the problem with boys – the reason they cannot become men on their own – is that they do not have any semen. Older men help them out by giving them their semen. These exchanges of bodily fluids have been termed "boy-inseminating rites,"[19] and take a variety of forms. In some groups, boys get semen from older boys and men by fellating them; in other groups, men have anal sex with the boys; and in still other groups, the gift of bodily fluids takes the form of semen being smeared on the boys who are being initiated into the world of adult men.[20]

Like the general situation among the ancient Greeks, these rituals might be considered to be a variety of age-structured or transgenerational homosexuality because the males who participate fulfill different roles depending on their ages, with the young boys receiving the semen in some way, and the older boys and men being the donors.

The boy-inseminating rites among the Sambia of the Eastern Highlands of Papua New Guinea have been extensively studied and interpreted by anthropologist Gilbert Herdt.[21] Herdt made a number of field trips to Papua New Guinea starting in 1974 to study the Sambian rituals and has published a great deal on the subject.[22] The Eastern Highlands of Papua New Guinea are a tough area in which to live, and the Sambians, a group of about 2,000 people, have survived despite "constant war ... treacherous terrain, awful weather, severe protein deficiency ... strong potential for starvation, no medical care other than that of shamans, and an acceptance of killing other humans."[23] And, intriguingly, the Sambian culture also includes rituals in which males have what Westerners would consider to be sex with each other. Contrary to the Western stereotype, these guys are hardly sissies. Also intriguingly, the Sambians, like the ancient Greeks, do not have either a word for or a category of homosexuality in the Western sense.[24] And yet, all the young males spend a considerable amount of time having sex with other males.

Sexual activity with other males is a *requirement* for Sambian men. This activity takes place starting when boys are between 7 and 10 years old, and ends, usually, when a man marries and fathers a child.[25] The boys are segregated from the rest of the social group for a period of some years (what society would not be improved by segregating its male teenagers?). During this time the younger boys regularly fellate the older boys and ingest their semen. As boys mature, they become the semen donors for the younger boys. "The Sambia prescriptive rule allows youths, aged fifteen and older, to inseminate younger initiates for years, until the older males marry and father a child …. With fatherhood, sexual relations with boys are to cease by ritual edict; the men's marriages and duties to their children would be compromised by boy relations …. This ideal life plan is borne out in all but a handful of men; however, the exceptions suggest that a few males do not or cannot make the transition from same-sex to opposite-sex erotic relations."[26] As men mature in this culture, they re-enter a society in which they are expected to marry a woman, have sex with her, and father children.

It is generally the case that Sambian men make a smooth transition to what would in Western terms be considered to be a heterosexual life. However, Herdt (along with co-author Robert Stoller) has described one Sambian who was somewhat different from other men in his group.[27] Like all the other men in his culture, Kalutwo had gone through the ritual initiation rites as a youth. Although he was afraid at first, he eventually became an avid participant in the rituals.[28] As an adult, Kalutwo was married four times, but none of his wives wound up staying with him for long. It seems as if Kalutwo, unlike nearly all the other men in his society, wanted to continue having sex with boys as an adult. Stoller and Herdt say that Kalutwo "would be a homosexual anywhere, independent of the culture's erotic customs."[29]

All Sambian males over the age of 7 or so participate in sexual activity with other males. A few of them love it, most of them just do it, and a few of them never enjoy it and give it up as soon as they are allowed to.[30] Are Sambian males homosexuals? Not in the usual Western sense. In fact, the Sambians' ritual initiation practices provide an excellent illustration of the idea that homosexual behavior and homosexual identity are very different things. Are Sambian men "gay"? The Western term does not even begin to describe the intricacies of Sambian life. To quote Gil Herdt, "we are dealing, in Melanesia, with one of the most complex and intricate sexual systems in culture that has ever evolved."[31]

Herdt again: "age-structured homosexuality nearly always involves the notion that the person will later marry and have children."[32] This is not necessarily true in transgendered homosexual relationships, nor in egalitarian. A well known example of transgendered homosexual relationships is found in a number of North American Indian groups. It seems likely that individuals who participate in transgendered homosexual relations in Native American traditions usually did not reproduce in the context of heterosexual marriage. In fact, the primary characteristic of this type of sexuality "in the native view was not its same-sex nature, but the fact that it was nonprocreative."[33]

The "Berdache" tradition. Neither the Sambians nor the ancient Greeks had words in their languages that correspond to the recent Western concept of "the homosexual." While, technically, this might also have been the case among native North American groups, some of these cultures did incorporate a concept of *a type of person* who was likely to be having sexual relationships with others of their own biological sex. However these traditions usually went well beyond same-sex eroticism and implied an entire way of life for its participants that included distinctive forms of dress and types of work. These customs collectively have been referred to by the term "berdache" – a French word borrowed from Persian – that itself has become contentious.[34] Some people continue to use the term and others reject it as an obvious colonial import. Berdache practices also are known as "two-spirit" traditions because people who participated in this way of life combined the spirits of males and females in what was often a distinctive third gender. To complicate things further, many Native American groups have their own indigenous – and various – terms for these individuals.

The berdache tradition refers to individuals who adopt social roles that are usually filled by people of the other biological sex. Thus, in many North American Indian cultures, some men adopt social roles that are typically filled by women, and in some groups women adopt social roles that are usually filled by men. These individuals dress like members of the opposite biological sex, do work that is usually that of the opposite biological sex, and sometimes even marry individuals who are the same sex they are (berdaches generally did not marry each other). These individuals in effect become a third gender that is neither man nor woman but something entirely unique.

Berdache traditions are quite widespread in Native American groups: "alternative gender roles were among the most widely shared features of North American societies. Male berdaches have been documented in over 155 tribes .... In about a third of these groups, a formal status also existed for females who undertook a man's lifestyle, becoming hunters, warriors, and chiefs."[35] Interestingly, people who enter into relationships with berdaches, even though they are having homosexual relationships, are not themselves members of a third gender – they are considered to be "regular" men or women. The berdache tradition is considered to be an example of transgendered homosexuality in that individuals who are a part of this tradition do not fulfill the usual gender role that is typically seen among individuals of their biological sex. Although many groups have this tradition, the number of individuals participating at any given time is not large. "In small groups, with populations of a few hundred, there might have been only one or two berdaches in a given generation. In larger communities, their numbers were sufficient for them to be recognized as a social group."[36]

How did individuals become part of this tradition? According to Will Roscoe, "the process by which third gender identity was adopted ... varied, but one dominant pattern emerges cross-culturally. Recognition of berdache orientation typically occurred when a boy showed interest and aptitude in women's work or a girl persistently engaged in the activities of boys and men."[37] In fact it seems generally to have been the case that what recent Western social scientists might call childhood gender nonconformity marked the early lives of individuals who were destined to follow the berdache way of life. Anthropologist Walter Williams says that berdachism is thought to be the reflection of a child's inborn character and "the consistency of reports from various culture areas over the centuries is amazing."[38] To quote one berdache about his childhood: "I knew I was different."[39] In 1919, another berdache told an interviewer that there had always been people like him, "they were born that way."[40]

※　◉　◉　◉　❦

Same-sex eroticism in ancient Greece, Melanesian boy-inseminating rituals, and the berdache tradition could be thought of as varying cultural manifestations of homosexual desire though they are really much more than that. These different cultural traditions mark out entirely different worlds, even if the actual behaviors involved seem to be similar to what is thought of as homosexuality in the modern West. The cultures are different though, and undoubtedly the behaviors mean different things to the participants. While they may resonate with recent Western homosexuality, none of these three traditions is truly the same as what recent Westerners think of as homosexuality.

All men of a certain class were expected to participate in male-male sexual relations in ancient Greece – as well as be married to women. *All* young men are expected to participate in the inseminating rituals among the Sambians during their youth. Like the gay minority in recent Euro-American cultures, just *some* individuals in some North American Indian cultures would have been expected to be a part of the berdache tradition. But unlike gay men in the West, the male berdache were not regarded simply as men, but rather were considered to be people who had a separate gender to themselves. Cultural diversity in homosexual behavior needs to be looked at from *within* its specific cultural milieu. The behaviors that are engaged in may be outwardly the same, but what do they mean to the participants? How do the participants interpret their own behavior? Would there have been men among the ancient Greeks who would have described themselves as homosexual if their language and culture had had such a word or concept? This seems to be supported by *The Symposium*. What about among the Sambians? Perhaps some men would rather continue the sexual way of life of their adolescent years all through their adult lives. That is not really an option though. What about the berdache? Perhaps some of those individuals would have embraced a homosexual identity. Are there now gay Native Americans fulfilling similar roles within Native American social groups? Possibly.[41]

Did people have the possibility of being "gay" in recent Western terms in these societies? Probably not. If a Greek man or a Sambian man felt "different" from his fellows, that feeling was irrelevant in most public ways. Their lives would likely include sex with both men and women nonetheless. Among the berdache, it seems as if similar feelings of "difference" might have been there but "difference" here would have been accompanied by a whole way of life, up to and including the adoption of a third gender. What about the partners of berdache – people not thought to be different from "regular" men or women, even though their spouses were of the same biological sex – did the partners of the berdache feel as youths that they were "different"?

Sexuality, according to the social constructionist paradigm, is subjective. But does that include object choice? Cultural diversity in sexuality, especially as among the ancient Greeks and the Sambians, does not seem to support the idea of an inborn sexual orientation to a particular sex. Or does it?

Most social scientists do not seem to be interested in looking at the interaction of biology and culture in the formation of humans. They are, by definition, not biologists. According to Will Roscoe, for example, "Clearly, sexual and gender diversity are an original part of the human heritage. It is not necessary to turn to theories of genetics and human biology to account for this."[42] Similarly, according to Evelyn Blackwood, "Although I do not deny the possibility of biophysical influences on human behavior, I want to pursue a social analysis further."[43] These are examples of what is probably a pretty common approach among cultural anthropologists and social scientists in general. That being, that there may be biological influences on human behavior but they choose to focus instead on cultural influences on behavior. They think it is not necessary to look toward biology for explanations of human behavior, and that doing so might run the risk of essentialism or – even worse – biological determinism.

It may not be necessary to look toward biological or genetic causation for sexual and gender variance as seen in North American Indian cultures and elsewhere. On the surface, simplistic discussions of a gene for homosexuality do not do justice to the variability in same-sex sexual activity that has been seen both historically and in different cultures throughout the world. The most common approach to sexual diversity among social scientists today is probably that "the evidence that homosexuality is a social construction is far more powerful than the evidence for a widespread organic predisposition toward homosexual desire."[44]

The absence in some cultures of what recent Western cultures have termed "the homosexual" seems to imply that there is no simple gene for homosexuality. If it were the case that a particular gene inevitably results in gay individuals, then gay people would probably be found in all cultures. But perhaps it is the possibility for *expression* of that gene that does not exist in many cultures. Is it possible that some people in every culture do have a gene for homosexuality? It looks *on the surface* like this cannot be true: not all cultures seem to have a subset of the population that is lesbian or gay. But that is just on the surface. What do we really know about sexual *desire* in other cultures? Anthropology cannot even begin to get at that topic. What if … there are people in every culture who *would be* gay if that culture included such a possibility? What if … every culture includes people who feel "different" when they are young but because of the constraints of their cultures never identify their feelings as what Westerners would term homoerotic? What if there is a gene for homosexuality that somehow makes people feel "different" when they are young and then sexually attracted to the same sex for the rest of their lives? Despite the evolutionary rules, it is not that far-fetched to believe that this could be the case.

In short, what if we were to look for biological or genetic causation in homosexuality? In some ways this would be most parsimonious, meaning that it might be the simplest explanation for diverse phenomena. For all our cultural diversity, we are, after all, members of one species. Perhaps anthropologists from a few generations back were right. Perhaps every human population has a small number of people in it that are predisposed toward an interest in sex with others of the same biological sex. Although the cross-cultural evidence *on its face* seems to indicate a variety of types of homosexual behavior and a variety of ways of expressing homosexual desire, the jury is out on whether or not this desire is something that some individuals feel in every society.

Just for argument's sake ... say there is homoerotic desire on the part of a small number of people in every social group. Say there is a genetic basis for homosexuality that results in this desire being felt and sometimes – though not always – being expressed. How might a gene for homosexuality evolve? That is the subject of Chapter Eight.

CHAPTER EIGHT

The Evolution of Homosexuality

I could see that M. de Charlus was about to tell us in what fashion these habits had evolved.

MARCEL PROUST, THE CAPTIVE[1]

Before launching into the topic of how a gay gene might have evolved, I would like to offer a brief definition. When referring to a gay gene, I am referring to a *hypothetical* sequence of DNA that exists within the human genome, the possession of which somehow results in an individual's being sexually attracted to members of their own biological sex.

The key word here is "somehow." Although developments in genetics – in particular recent advances in molecular genetics – have been extraordinary, there remains something of a giant black box between what scientists do know for certain (sequences of base pairs in DNA), and what many people *think* scientists know for certain (particular DNA sequences invariably result in particular traits, either physical or behavioral). Put simply, DNA sequences code for proteins, they do not code for traits. How proteins develop into living organisms is less well known. And how those proteins could conceivably result in an individual human being who is sexually oriented towards their own biological sex is an utter mystery.

So much has been learned so rapidly in the field of genetics that I do not want to be too skeptical about whether or not or how quickly this mystery might be unraveled. The whole story of development from DNA to person might be known in my lifetime (I am planning to live a long time). But it seems generally that the technology of DNA sequencing has raced way ahead of scientists' abilities to make use of the data they are collecting.[2] In her brief but compelling history of genetics in the twentieth century, science historian Evelyn Fox Keller writes that even if there were "a simple correspondence between one gene and one protein, we would still have to bridge the gap between proteins and organism: how can an organism be built out of the mere accumulation of different proteins?"[3] The deciphering of an organism's genome is an important step – a step that has been completed for a number of species – but it is important also to think of "sequence data as a tool, as a way of probing the complexity of developmental dynamics."[4]

Even though no one can begin to explain how a gay gene might lead to the development of an actual gay person, many people are of the opinion that a gay gene exists. But no one can speak definitively on this topic. For now, a gay gene is a hypothetical construct, something that might exist. Fortunately for the purposes of this chapter, the proof of such a gene's actual existence is not required in a discussion of its evolution. Sociobiologists frequently discuss the evolution of hypothetical genes, and occasionally even discuss the evolution of genes for homosexuality. It is important to remember though that such discussions are not meant to be taken literally. There may or may not be an actual sequence of DNA in the human genome that somehow "makes" people gay.

The biological evidence that gay people are genetically or anatomically different in some way from straight people has been increasing in recent years as this question has been explored by scientists who are using more and more sophisticated techniques. Nevertheless, the evidence for biological difference is not much more than *suggestive* that variations in sexual orientation are influenced by biology. Perhaps the strongest evidence that gay people are born that way comes from unscientific individual life stories. Many lesbians and gay men retrospectively identify an interest in their own biological sex going back to childhood – often well before they were aware that homosexuality existed, and often well before they were able to comprehend sexuality.

In an article from the national lesbian and gay magazine *The Advocate*, for example, 16 people were interviewed about their feelings about the roots of their sexual orientation, among other things.[5] Although the respondents were of varying ages and backgrounds, their ideas about why it is that they are gay were remarkably consistent: "I was born gay"; "I think it's most definitely genetics"; "I've known since I was 4"; "I think it's biological." Just one person in the *Advocate* survey thought "being gay is a combination of environment and genetics." One person who identifies as bisexual "always felt different."

While this article is in itself hardly definitive or scientific, it is interesting, and perhaps significant when considering the existence of a hypothetical gay gene. Of course, the *Advocate*'s editors might have presented a highly selective set of responses in this article. That is, they might have *chosen* to include a large majority of respondents who felt that homosexuality was something that was with them from birth or early childhood. Studies have shown that the American population at large is less apt to be homophobic if they believe that homosexuality is biologically based rather than a choice.[6] Perhaps the editors at the *Advocate* are playing that angle somewhat when they present life stories that seem to support the idea that homosexuality is innate. (Of course whether it is innate or something people choose whimsically should not matter at all, but apparently it does make a difference to many people.)

You could also argue that the recollections of the people who were interviewed might be suspect: childhood memories are often quite fuzzy. Each of the people interviewed is openly gay – so openly gay that their life stories and their photographs have been published in a national lesbian and gay newsmagazine. Perhaps saying "I was gay from birth" is a form of self-affirmation in a homophobic world. Perhaps also some of the gay people who say that they were gay from birth are aware that straight people are likely to be positively swayed in their opinions of gay people if the gay people "can't help themselves," rather than if they have *chosen* to love people of the same sex.

Perhaps. But perhaps many straight people would also say that they were aware of their sexual orientation from an early age. This could be dismissed as a reflection of the omnipresence of heterosexual role models, or we could just run with the idea that an individual's particular sexual orientation is something that is likely to have been genetically influenced and thus with people in some form from their earliest childhood. So, do individuals have an innate sexual orientation? That question remains unanswerable, but for the purposes of this chapter I am going to assume that they do. I am going to assume that the common sentiment among gay people that they were "born that way" is a reflection of an innate, possibly genetic, predisposition toward homosexuality that some people are born with. (I would consider a trait to be innate if that trait reliably develops in essentially any natural environment.) In effect, I am using as a model the recent Western version of a human group in which the majority of people are straight, and a minority are gay. Generalizing from Western cultures to humanity as a whole may be questionable, if not offensive, to many cultural anthropologists and social theorists.[7]

The cross-cultural evidence that some people in every social group are sexually oriented towards others of the same sex is, I would argue, ambiguous. On the surface, it seems as if the anthropological evidence *does not* support the idea that sexual orientation is something that is innate. There is a great deal of variability in how sexuality is experienced in different cultures. Among the ancient Greeks where men were expected to be bisexual, most men followed cultural expectations. Similarly in many Melanesian cultures where men are expected to have sex with each other for years at a time but then give it up and marry women, nearly all men follow cultural expectations. Among many groups of Native Americans, men and women who followed the berdache tradition had life histories that were similar to those of many recent Western lesbians and gay men – at least in terms of what was often a lifelong focus on relationships with people of the same sex. But of course, berdaches gave up their expected genders to follow this tradition, which is not something lesbians and gay men in recent Western cultures have generally been asked to do.

Despite cultural variability in the expression of homosexuality, I would argue that this variability in itself cannot be used as evidence that there is not a gay gene, in that the anthropological record is essentially silent on the question of *desire*. It appears *on the surface* that there cannot be a simple gay gene that invariably results in people who only have sex with others of the same sex. In some cultures, homosexuality is an unknown phenomenon. However, are there individuals in those cultures who would like to have homosexual relationships but who are thwarted by cultures in which this is not a recognized possibility? Perhaps if homosexuality is not a viable option, heterosexuality is the only way to proceed. Even in recent Western cultures where homosexuality is a generally known option, many people deny their homosexual desires because those desires are stigmatized. Perhaps there are some people everywhere who have a gay gene.

A gene for homosexuality is, at best, hypothetical. But if there is such a thing, human cultures provide something of an explanation for the apparent conundrum of that gene's survival in the human species. The conundrum is less of a mystery than it appears to be: when taking into account the history of the human species and the universal appearance of marriage in all cultures, it would seem that gay genes might owe their survival to the cultural rules that prescribe heterosexual marriage for all or almost all adults. Gay genes might have been passed through innumerable generations of people because the people who have them have nonetheless been married and reproducing – cultural rules have insisted that they do so.

The near universality of heterosexual marriage in traditional societies takes quite a bit of the conundrum out of the evolutionary survival of gay genes. If there is a gay gene that some people have, and if those people are nevertheless married to people of the opposite sex, gay genes are likely to persist.[8] If traditional societies marry off all or nearly all eligible individuals of reproductive age, whether or not someone has a gay gene is, in a way, irrelevant. The person with that gene is likely to be married to someone of the opposite sex whether he or she wants to be or not. That person is likely to reproduce despite their gay gene.

There is something of an ironic implication in this argument. People who preach family values seem to want everyone – no exceptions – to live married heterosexual lives, with no sex outside of marriage and no homosexuality. But married heterosexual lives are conceivably what has kept genes for homosexuality alive over the course of human history. Ironically it would seem that the best way to ensure the survival of genes for homosexuality might be to make everyone get married to people of the opposite sex. Now there is a conundrum for the proponents of family values.[9]

The premise of this book is that gay genes are not likely to evolve or survive if those genes invariably result in their owners having sex only with others of the same biological sex. Same-sex couplings cannot, in and of themselves, produce offspring. While this sounds like it might be a homophobic premise, I think that in fact it is simply logical. I am not questioning the desirability of gay genes, or by implication the desirability of gay people. I am instead pointing out what is essentially a logical issue. A gene for homosexuality is unlikely to be maintained in a naturally reproducing population. In the case of the human species though, it is at least conceivable that just such a gene does exist. And its survival may in fact have been predicated upon human cultures having rules that require marriage. Humans, I would suggest, are not a naturally reproducing species in that whether or not and with whom an individual has sex is often influenced by cultural expectations and rules. If there is a gay gene in the human species it might have survived because cultural rules prescribe marriage for all.

Most of the explanations that sociobiologists have proposed to explain the existence of gay genes consider only the genes themselves as theoretical constructs and do not take into account that there is little evidence of genes for homosexuality in other species, and the direct biological evidence for a human gay gene is tenuous. They also usually do not give enough weight to the history and cultures of *Homo sapiens*. I would argue that it is essential to emphasize human cultures in this question, and will explore further the particular history and demography of the human species later in this chapter.

Before looking at sociobiological suggestions regarding the evolution of homosexuality, I would first like to mention a couple of semantic points. When writing about the "evolution" of a gay gene, it is not so much the original *emergence* of the gene that is of interest. Any trait can appear in a species through mutation. Indeed, mutations provide the raw material for evolution. When I am talking about the "evolution of homosexuality" or the "evolution of a gay gene," I am actually talking about the *maintenance* of that trait in the human species. Anything can appear once; if there is a gay gene in the human species, the conundrum is that the gene seems to be common and seems to have survived over generations.

A second semantic point, which might mostly be of interest to biologists, is that the phrase "gay gene" is *shorthand* in that people all, technically, have the same genes, but different variants of those genes are found in different individuals. An example should clarify this. People all have genes for eye color. Those genes can specify brown or blue or something else. Brown and blue are *alleles* or forms of a gene for eye color. Similarly, assuming that all humans have "genes for sexual orientation," there could be a homosexual allele and a heterosexual allele. Technically, this book is about the survival of an allele that produces people who are sexually oriented towards others of the same biological sex. The phrase "evolution of a gay gene" is used as shorthand to simplify the discussion.

Evolution by natural selection was discussed at some length in Chapters Two and Three. It was suggested there that the behavior of modern humans has been shaped by our long history as a biological species that, like every other species, has been subject to evolutionary pressures. Darwin's concept of natural selection explains the mechanism by which evolution occurs: living things vary and because of these variations some individuals have an advantage in competition for scarce resources. The winners reproduce more and their genes are passed along to future generations.

The field of sociobiology explicitly applies Darwin's ideas to the evolution of social behavior among all species, including humans. In particular, sociobiologists look at the behavior of individuals and how those behaviors help and hinder reproduction. Nearly all sociobiologists agree that natural selection focuses on *individuals* rather than on *groups*. While it might not be difficult to see how something like homosexuality might evolve for the good of a social group, this type of thinking is not consonant with sociobiology's basic tenet that individual reproduction is the metaphorical goal of living things.[10]

Because a gay gene would theoretically result in an individual not reproducing at all, the mere existence of such a thing is rather mystifying. Most sociobiological explanations for homosexuality posit some sort of advantage conferred by a gay gene that more or less counterbalances the idea that a gay gene is less likely to be reproduced than a gene for heterosexuality. G.E. Hutchinson published what was probably the earliest discussion of how a gene for homosexuality might have evolved in 1959.[11] Hutchinson noted that some people exhibit paraphilias, or tendencies to focus their sexuality on "goals which cannot lead to reproduction, in the place of … partner[s] of the opposite sex."[12] Paraphilias, including homosexuality and what Hutchinson called "fetichism," are puzzling from an evolutionary perspective. It is possible (although even Hutchinson himself did not seem to think it very likely) that people who exhibit paraphilias have a double dose of a gene for that behavior. A single copy of that gene in any given individual will not have the same effect. There is precedent for this, and in fact there is a term in genetics for exactly this type of situation: a gene for homosexuality, by this line of reasoning, might be maintained in a population because of something called heterozygote advantage.

A heterozygote is an individual who has two *different* forms of a particular gene, one of which was inherited from mom, the other from dad. (A homozygote, by contrast, has two essentially identical forms of the same gene, one inherited from each parent.) Say, for argument's sake, that sexual orientation is determined by one gene (this is an argument that virtually no one would make). If H represents the dominant heterosexual gene, and h represents the recessive homosexual gene, the pairs of genes in any individual could be HH, Hh, or hh. If the Hh individuals have some advantage by virtue of their being heterozygous (having one copy of each form of the gene), then the h gene is likely to remain in the population, even if the hh individuals do not reproduce. This is heterozygote advantage.

It is thought that some real (as opposed to hypothetical) genes act this way. For example, there are two forms for the hemoglobin gene, called A and S. The A form of the gene codes for round red blood cells, and the S gene codes for sickle-shaped red blood cells. Individuals who are homozygous for the S version of the hemoglobin gene (who are "SS" for that trait) suffer from sickle cell anemia and might not live long enough to reproduce. But individuals who are heterozygotes – who have both the A form and the S form of this gene – are less likely to suffer from malaria; they are "partially protected against the most dangerous form of malaria, falciparum malaria."[13] Thus it is thought that the S form of the gene is maintained in the population because it provides an advantage to individuals who have it – as long as they have it *along with* an A gene. "Scientists suspect that the relatively high frequencies of genes that cause a number of other genetic diseases may also be the result of heterozygote advantage."[14]

Although heterozygote advantage certainly seems to be at the root of the maintenance of some evolutionarily puzzling genes within the human genome, there is actually no evidence that a gene for a homosexual orientation might be among them. Homosexuality, although it is thought to run in families, does not seem to follow a simple pattern of dominant and recessive genes. Also, something as complex as sexual orientation is not generally thought to be something that could be "determined" by a single gene. Nonetheless, the important point to take from G.E. Hutchinson is that a gene for homosexuality might have some sort of advantage that balances out the fact that a homosexual person will leave no offspring if they never have sex with someone of the opposite sex.

This idea – that a gay gene might have a positive evolutionary impact – is also the basis for the suggestion that a gene for homosexuality could be maintained in a species by kin selection. Kin selection as a possible explanation for the evolutionary origins of homosexuality was discussed earlier. In 1975, biologist E.O. Wilson suggested in his very influential book *Sociobiology*[15] that

> "The [male] homosexual members of primitive societies may have functioned as helpers, either while hunting in company with other men or in more domestic occupations at the dwelling sites. Freed from the special obligations of parental duties, they could have operated with special efficiency in assisting close relatives. Genes favoring homosexuality could then be sustained at a high equilibrium level by kin selection alone."[16]

(It is interesting to ponder how common it is for the heterosexual males of the human species to really experience "the special obligations of parental duties." But that is another book.)

Wilson's point is that if you look at evolution from the viewpoint of the propagation of particular genes, and if you keep in mind that related people share genes, then an individual who helps his kin raise their offspring is in effect helping to propagate his own genes too – because his little nieces and nephews have many of the same genes he does. Blood is thicker than water, and genes want to be propagated by any means necessary.

Wilson is a specialist in the behavior of social insects. Within that group of species, there have in fact evolved non-reproductive castes of insects that devote their lives to helping their kin reproduce – but who, themselves, forego reproduction. "In these insects apparent self-sacrifice reaches the point where large numbers of individuals are completely sterile; they never reproduce themselves but instead spend their whole adult lives devoted to rearing the young of others."[17] (Non-reproductive worker ants do not remind me of gay people but perhaps I am not all that open minded about ants.)

Another example of kin selection that is relatively widespread in nature is a phenomenon known as "helper at the nest,"[18] something that is seen regularly in some species of birds and mammals. Birds, which are generally rather monogamous, lay clutches of eggs and the resulting offspring eventually fledge, or fly off to start their own families. Sometimes a juvenile or two will not leave home as soon as they might, and instead will stick around to help their parents raise the next set of offspring. The young that stay around are called helpers at the nest, and it is thought that they may be contributing to their own genetic legacy by helping raise other individuals with whom they share many genes. Even if a helper does not reproduce himself, the siblings he is helping to raise carry some of the helper's genes.

While it is not inconceivable that kin selection could be at the root of homosexuality in humans, it is worth noting that in both the social insects and in species in which the helper at the nest phenomenon is seen, the individuals who are helping their kin reproduce are not homosexual. They are generally asexual. From an evolutionary perspective, asexuality makes sense in this context. At least in comparison with asexuality, homosexuality, if anything, would seemingly diminish the likelihood that gay individuals would be of assistance to their families. A celibate sibling might be helpful in terms of kin selection, as they are in some species of birds and insects. A homosexual sibling is probably not hanging around the house.

Furthermore, from the perspective of an individual with a gay gene, the help that person would have to provide to their family in order to make it worth their while to forego reproduction altogether would have to be really substantial.[19] It is easier and certainly more direct to reproduce yourself. If that is impossible for some reason, then helping kin reproduce is a good evolutionary fallback. In the place where helping has seemingly evolved to a great extent, among the social insects, the organisms also are different from humans and other mammals in a very significant way: non-reproducing social insects, because of a genetic quirk, actually share ¾ of their DNA, as compared to ½ of their DNA as found in mammals. This makes it considerably more likely that kin selection will work among the social insects.

Is there any evidence from modern humans that kin selection might be at the root of the evolution of homosexuality? You would predict that if kin selection were significant in the evolution of a gay gene, then gay people might be helpful in some way to their biological families and that that help would have a positive impact on their families' overall reproduction. At least one study has looked at this issue in a modern population and found that

> "Homosexual men were no more likely than heterosexual men to channel resources toward family members. Indeed, heterosexual men tended to give more financial resources to siblings

than homosexual men. Furthermore, homosexual men were somewhat more estranged from family members, especially from fathers and oldest siblings."[20]

Of course, a lack of support for kin selection in one time and one place is not definitive. It is possible that a gay gene may have evolved millions of years ago and could conceivably have been maintained in the species by kin selection, even if that does not work any longer. (In fact, it is important generally to keep in mind that genes for something or another might have been "for" something else entirely at another point in the evolution of *Homo sapiens*.[21])

The real test of whether or not kin selection is at the root of the evolution of a gay gene would be to see if kin selection seems to be acting in hunter-gatherer societies. Hunting and gathering was the method of making a living throughout most of the evolution of the human species, up until the development of agriculture in a few different areas of the world around 10,000 years ago. Very few people still live by hunting and gathering today, and those that do so are not and cannot be considered to be exact stand-ins for ancestral humans. Without a viable time machine though, anthropologists who are interested in the history of the human species try to extrapolate from modern hunter-gatherer societies to humans from the distant past. While there is some homosexual behavior, very little homosexuality as a way of life in the recent Western sense is seen in hunter-gatherer societies.[22] Thus, there is little support among modern hunter-gatherers for the idea that kin selection might be at the root of the evolution of homosexuality in humans.

Although there is not any obvious evidence from cross-cultural studies by anthropologists to support the idea that kin selection is at the root of the evolution of homosexuality, a variant on kin selection proposed by James Weinrich does take human cultures into account, and has a different emphasis than the kin selection theory as such.

Sociobiologist James Weinrich suggested an explanation for the evolution of homosexuality in humans that was similar to, but more subtle than, the kin selection hypothesis suggested by E.O. Wilson. Weinrich was elaborating upon a brief suggestion made by R.L. Trivers in 1974 in a paper called "Parent-offspring conflict."[23] Trivers pointed out that although parents and their offspring share genes and thus have *similar* interests from an evolutionary perspective, related individuals are nonetheless not identical and thus their interests will not be identical. Conflicts between parents and offspring should therefore be expected in many areas. It could be in the evolutionary interests of parents to have a homosexual child:

> "Parents subconsciously determine that it would be better for them, in terms of getting a larger number of copies of their genes into subsequent generations, if their family focused its reproductive and survival resources on the offspring of certain of their children but not others. Having made this determination, parents behave toward certain of their children in such ways that these children become homosexual."[24]

(Can an individual's parents make him or her gay? With all due respect to Sigmund Freud, this seems considerably less likely to me than the idea that there might be a gay gene.)

This "parental manipulation" theory of homosexuality is similar to the more general kin selection explanation in that in both instances the homosexual people are, in some sense, being gay in order to be helpful to their blood relatives. They are sacrificing their own reproduction in order to assist their genetic lineages. Thus a gay gene could be maintained in a population because the families in which that gene is found, on the whole, reproduce at a good rate, even though some individuals within the family do not reproduce at all.

Inspired by these related ideas that homosexuality might represent reproductive altruism – in this case individuals being altruistic to their kin by *not* reproducing – James Weinrich suggested in 1987[25] that the variants on this theory of the evolution of homosexuality have in common the idea that the gay people do not reproduce at all. A complete sacrifice of individual reproduction seems to be a very high cost for an individual to pay. In order for it to be genetically worthwhile for an individual to completely forego reproduction, that individual would have to be of considerable assistance to their families. Weinrich's idea was that the survival of a gene for homosexuality would be considerably less puzzling if the individuals who have that gene are nonetheless reproducing. He suggested that in that case, "the magnitude of the altruism is much reduced."[26] This idea would be applicable to "societies in which social pressures require marriage of essentially all reproductively able individuals."[27]

In 1997, Jim McKnight published a book on the subject of the evolution of homosexuality[28] in which he suggested a variation on the idea that a gay gene might be maintained in the human species by heterozygote advantage. Again, this concept essentially suggests that there is an advantage to having a gay gene along with a straight gene, and because this combination is advantageous, the gay gene is maintained in the population even though people who have a double dose of the gay gene might not reproduce. McKnight's contribution was that he speculated on exactly what the advantages of having a gay gene might be for people who have it along with a straight gene. So, "it is probable that a gene for male homosexuality confers an immediate reproductive advantage by directly enhancing sex drive or some other aspect of sexual performance."[29] Consider a straight man who is genetically Hh: he has one homosexual gene (h) in combination with a heterosexual gene (H). If that man has a lot of sex with women and therefore reproduces more than men who are genetically either entirely heterosexual (HH) or entirely homosexual (hh), then the h gene will be maintained in the population.

McKnight pursues this line of reasoning further when he suggests that straight men who have one gay gene might be more appealing to women, and women might be more likely to choose to marry and have children with these "homosexually-enabled straight men."[30] Such men who have "access to both masculine and feminine traits will be able to offer sensitivity, creativity and better communication skills in addition to the traditional male offerings."[31] (Whereas homosexually impoverished straight men offer ... the same old inarticulate insensitivity?)

McKnight concludes that "homosexuality is an evolutionary byproduct, part of our variable sexual orientation and held in balance against its deleterious consequences by selecting for enhanced heterosexuality."[32] McKnight's theory is intriguing but based, ultimately, on stereotypes about male behavior (both straight and gay) that might be little more than artifacts of recent Western cultures and prejudices. Furthermore, "there is currently no empirical evidence to support such postulated mechanisms in the context of the evolution of homosexual orientation."[33]

There are two more, related theories about the origins of homosexuality in the human species that I would like to mention. These two theories suggest social functions for homosexuality in human evolution. Frank Muscarella has suggested that a propensity toward what might be termed bisexuality is a feature of the human species as a whole, and suggests that this might have evolved from a tendency in primate groups for adolescent individuals to live peripherally to the rest of the social group. If these peripheral adolescents were disposed toward homoerotic behavior, that behavior "may have served as a mechanism of affiliation which reinforced and strengthened [their] relationships …. The social assistance of peers and higher status companions may have increased the likelihood of access to resources and may have provided allies to help ward off attacks" from others of the same species.[34]

Similarly, R.C. Kirkpatrick[35] has suggested that homosexual behavior may have evolved because of reciprocal altruism. Robert Trivers's concept of reciprocal altruism[36] suggests that individuals will treat each other well if they have the expectation that the other individual will in turn be nice to them at some future date. Kirkpatrick suggests that "same-sex alliances have reproductive advantages, and sexual behavior at times maintains these alliances."[37] These alliances may have been a key aspect of the evolution of the human species.

One more idea about the evolution of a gene for homosexuality that should be mentioned has been proposed in conjunction with the research on gay genes that was carried out by Dean Hamer and his colleagues. Recall that Hamer found evidence for a possible gay gene on the X chromosome in men. The fact that the gene was on the X chromosome is intriguing from an evolutionary perspective. Genes on the X chromosome are a particularly interesting part of the human genome because the X chromosome, along with the Y chromosome, determine an individual's biological sex. Human females have two X chromosomes and males have one X chromosome and one Y chromosome. Because men have only one X chromosome, there are some genetic traits that are much more frequently manifested in men than in women. More specifically, if there is a recessive gene for a particular trait found on an X chromosome, a man would express that trait because he has only one copy of that gene on his one and only X chromosome. A woman, by contrast, *might* express that trait, but likely will not because she has two X chromosomes and even if one of those X's has a recessive gene, it may be masked by a dominant gene on her other X chromosome.

Thus men more often exhibit what are known as sex-linked or X-linked traits.

A few of these traits are rather well known. Color blindness and hemophilia are both sex-linked, i.e., they are seen more often in men than in women. Genes for color blindness and genes for hemophilia are found on the X chromosome. A man who has one of these genes will express the trait in question whereas a woman who has one of these genes probably will not express the trait because the recessive gene that would cause hemophilia or color blindness is very likely to be masked by a dominant gene on her *other* X chromosome. Although she does not express the trait, she is a carrier of that trait and can pass the recessive gene along to her offspring.

Say, for argument's sake, that there is a gene on the X chromosome that somehow results (again, the key word being somehow) in an individual who really, really likes to have sex with men. From an evolutionary perspective this might be a good thing for a woman – she might wind up having more children than a woman who is less enthralled by sex with men. But if this gene is contained in the X chromosome of a man, and if he really, really likes having sex with men, it is quite possible that he will not be passing his genes along to future generations.

Interestingly, strictly from the perspective of this gene for homosexuality on the X chromosome, it might not matter that a man with this gene does not reproduce – *as long as* women with this gene reproduce more – as long as women with this gene reproduce enough to make up for the fact that their male relatives who have the same gene do not reproduce.[38] It is conceivable that enhanced female reproduction could account for the evolution of a gene for homosexuality on the X chromosome and it is intriguing that it was in this area of the human genome that Hamer's team met with success in their attempts to find a gene that is correlated with homosexual orientation. A recent survey of gay men in Italy also provides some support for this evolutionary scenario.[39] In that study, gay men reported both that they had more gay relatives on their mother's side of the family, and also that their maternal relatives produced a greater than expected number of offspring.

＃　◎　◎　◎　~

Each of the theories and their variations on the subject of the evolution of a gene for homosexuality discussed above are plausible from an evolutionary perspective – biologically plausible, but perhaps not very likely from a practical perspective. One thing that complicates all of these scenarios is that there might be a time lag effect at work here: a gene for homosexuality might be something that originally appeared in the human genome a very long time ago when much was different about human life.

If you consider the basic kin selection hypothesis, for example, it seems rather unlikely from our current vantage point that kin selection is maintaining a gene for homosexuality in the human species. Indeed, it is not just unlikely, it is actually somewhat offensive: so many gay people in our homophobic society are estranged from their families of origin it could almost be thought of as outrageous that kin selection – in this case the idea that gay people are helping their biological families reproduce – is at work in America in the third millennium.

But of course just because kin selection seems unlikely at this point in the history of the human species, that does not rule out the possibility that kin selection is at the root of the maintenance of a gene for homosexuality over evolutionary time. America circa 2,000 C.E. is just one data point from an evolutionary perspective. And it is one rather unique data point at that. Similarly, the other evolutionary theories on the origins and maintenance of a gene for homosexuality all seem plausible if you keep in mind that a gene for homosexuality may be something that evolved in the distant past.

Sociobiologists are often well aware that the behavior of modern humans might be a reflection of the environment in which humans evolved, rather than something that is good for individual reproduction right now. This complicates things considerably because instead of being able to study people behaving in the here and now in ways that might help or hinder their reproduction, sociobiologists sometimes need to speculate on the utility of human behaviors in the past in order to make sense of the present. While this speculation can be dismissed as something that is less than scientific, on the whole, I think the storytelling of sociobiology is a positive thing. While sociobiology generally is not nearly as rigorous as physics, it does create a big picture that puts behavior in context. That context is evolution by natural selection. How we behave now generally jibes with how natural selection suggests organisms should behave. And when our behavior does not jibe with expectations, that too is interesting from an evolutionary perspective. Perhaps much of human behavior seen today would have been adaptive or good for reproduction in the distant past.

But homosexuality? The sociobiological theories on the evolution of homosexuality are not all that compelling. Homosexuality just does not make sense from an evolutionary perspective. Nevertheless, I think it is possible that there is a gay gene in the human species and I think it is possible that that gene has not just survived against the odds but indeed has flourished. But you have to consider the impact of human cultures (in particular the universality of heterosexual marriage in traditional societies) and the unique history and demography of the human species to come up with a plausible story about how a gay gene might have evolved.

Here is a scenario.

While it may sound homophobic to say that a gay gene should not be maintained in a naturally reproducing population, I had suggested earlier in this chapter that this idea is inspired here less by homophobia than by logic. I also suggested that the human species might not actually be a naturally reproducing species because people are expected to follow cultural rules, in particular rules that suggest that everyone must marry someone of the opposite sex. In short, if there was a gay gene that some people had way back in time, that gene likely survived because the people who had it were still reproducing.

Although no one can say for sure what human social groups were like in the distant past, let's say for argument's sake that humans lived in small bands of related males. Females moved between groups at puberty to pair off in marriage-like arrangements with the males. This is not implausible since it is essentially the format for social groups in the closest relatives of the human species, the common chimpanzees and bonobos, with a key difference being that chimpanzees do not pair bond for long periods of time as humans tend to do. Presumably at some point in human evolution, pair bonding between males and females became the most common mating system in the human species. If a gene for homosexuality evolved at any point *after that*, the gene would have been maintained if the individuals who have it are in culturally sanctioned – or culturally imposed – marriages with individuals of the opposite biological sex.[40]

There is another important demographic consideration that should be added to this scenario. For most of its existence, the human species extracted a living from its environment by hunting and gathering. Although some hunter-gatherer societies have had fairly high population densities, most surviving hunter-gatherer peoples – and presumably most human ancestors – live or have lived at relatively low population densities.

Why is population density significant? If there is a gene for homosexuality, it is conceivable that through most of human history the individuals who have had such a gene have gone through their lives being rather unlikely to encounter other individuals who also had that gene. They may have felt themselves to be different, but that difference went unnamed and essentially unnoticed in their cultures. Say, hypothetically, 4% of the human population has a gay gene.[41] If there is a human social group that consists of 100 people, 4 of those people have that gene. Say two of these people are female and two of them are male. Chances are good that these two women either will be of very different ages or they might be related to each other. The same situation will exist for the two men. Chances are very good that all four of these people will be married to individuals of the opposite sex. Chances are that even if these two women or these two men find each other and are attracted to each other they still will not be setting up house together and declaring their homosexual life partnership in a culture in which that is not a recognized possibility.

Thus, the demography of the human species might also have contributed to the survival of gay genes. Groups of people living at low densities are unlikely to produce a subculture of homosexuals, especially since some cultures do not recognize the possibility that two people of the same sex can be joined together in a sexual relationship akin to marriage.

The demography of the human species is also significant in another way when you are considering the evolution of a gene for homosexuality. In the last 10,000 years, roughly since the development of agriculture, the human population has skyrocketed, doubling at predictable intervals.[42] "The close association between population growth and the spread of agriculture leaves little doubt that the two developments were related, but which came first and what initiated the process are controversial."[43] Natural selection, which is a ruthless force in most circumstances, probably has not been as harsh a foe in the recent evolution of the human species. Since the development of agriculture, humans seem to have found an extraordinary niche. This niche has been such that genes that might not have survived under more ruthless conditions have survived in the past 10,000 years. And indeed, some of them have become quite prevalent.

Thanks to the human population explosion, very large numbers of humans now live very closely together at high densities. If there is a gay gene, individuals who have it are probably numerous and are living in a world in which they can find each other to an extent not before seen in human history. It is no accident that visible subcultures of homosexuals began emerging in large cities with high population densities. In a group of 100 people, someone with a gay gene is likely to be something of an anomaly. In a city of a million people, tens of thousands of gay people are much more likely to find each other.

To revisit the debate over essentialism versus social constructionism, it is interesting to note that whatever the differences between these two academic camps might be, the idea that demography plays a role in the evolution of homosexuality is something that people from both these perspectives might well agree on.[44] It is hard to be a self-actualized homosexual if you are the only one in town. It is not impossible, but it is easier to be gay if it is a recognized aspect of one's society, if there is a name for it. And it is much more likely to be a recognized aspect of society in larger social groups.

Is there a gay gene? Possibly. If there is a gay gene it might have survived – indeed it might have flourished – because of a combination of biological, cultural and demographic factors. In particular, the demography of the human species provides an explanation for why a gene for homosexuality might have survived among humankind: it has only been with the relatively recent concentration of large numbers of individuals into not very large areas that homosexual subcultures have been able to develop and individuals have become less tied to traditional heterosexual marriage. Since gay subcultures have appeared fairly predictably with urbanization, this does seem to support the idea that a homosexual preference is an innate aspect of some people's lives. Gay subcultures are unlikely to spring up out of nowhere. Unless you think that homosexuality is some kind of expression of evil or a pathological result of overcrowding in densely populated areas, it seems more likely that a gay gene has recently found an opportunity for expression because people are living at high densities and this concentration of people makes it possible for people with gay genes to find each other.

Again, I take it as significant that many American lesbians and gay men – at least those of us who came of age before homosexuality was all over the mass media – have similar stories to tell about feeling "different" when we were children. This difference is often retrospectively defined as a homosexual orientation. In a way, each individual who comes to a gay identity by this path is re-enacting the broader cultural emergence of homosexuality. Writ small, it is called coming out. Writ large, it is a cultural phenomenon.

This book is about an apparent conundrum: the unlikely survival of a gene for homosexuality. My context for looking at this question is that of sociobiology: a field that suggests that much as the physical forms of living things are shaped by natural selection, behaviors are also influenced by the same evolutionary forces. I think that the sociobiological paradigm is a powerful one, even if it does not satisfactorily explain the existence of homosexuality. And I think that a holistic sociobiology that incorporates human cultures and human demography can provide a valuable perspective on homosexuality, a trait that by the logic of evolution alone should not have evolved.

Unfortunately, sociobiology is not as popular in the American social sciences as it should be. There are many reasons why sociobiology is frowned upon. The main reason, I think, is that exploring the biological basis for behavior – human behavior in particular – strikes many liberal academics (and most American academics are liberals) as both deterministic and reductionistic. In fact some sociobiologists are probably guilty of both of these crimes. Nevertheless, there should be a place for an evolutionary perspective in American thought. There will be more on this topic as we conclude this tour of the unlikely evolution of homosexuality in Chapter Nine.

CHAPTER NINE

Homo sapiens in the Twenty-First Century

The force of circumstances is stronger than any individual, personal force just as the general tendencies in us are stronger than our personal inclinations.

IVAN TURGENEV, LITERARY REMINISCENCES[1]

There were signs up in my neighborhood that a leftist organization was having a meeting and the discussion topic for the evening was whether human nature is a barrier to socialism. I was thinking that the short answer to that question is "yes," but I decided to go to the meeting to see what the socialists thought. The meeting was held in a local church (what would Karl Marx have said to that?), and was attended by about 30 people, the majority of whom were young and earnest and prone to quoting Marx. They also mostly seemed to know each other. I was a stranger to their group, still rather earnest for someone in middle age, and prone to quoting Darwin.

The person who spoke first on the topic was something of a surprise, not because he was anything but young, earnest, and Marx-quoting, but rather because he dispensed with the evening's discussion topic so rapidly. It turned out that the answer was quite simple: human nature is *not* a barrier to socialism because there is no such thing as human nature. What we think of as human nature – the tendency for people to be greedy, selfish and uncooperative – is nothing more than an artifact of our having been raised in a capitalist society. Capitalism makes people greedy, selfish and uncooperative. It isn't always like that. It doesn't have to be like that. The end.

When the first speaker finished, I knew I would have to respond but before I had a chance to, another young, earnest Marxist spoke up and told the assembled group that sociobiologists, people who believe in human nature, are particularly evil, some of them going so far as to claim that rape is "natural." (I knew what she was referring to and in fact that work is not among sociobiology's shining moments.) At that point I got a word in. I said I felt like I had to "out" myself as a person who believes in sociobiology and the relevance of evolutionary theory to the lives of humans. I tried to explain that humans are primates, animals who have evolved over millions of years, and that we still have a great deal in common with monkeys and other apes, in terms of behavior. In fact quite often people seem to be little more than upright walking apes in suits. The thing about capitalism, I said, is that it does encourage people to be greedy, selfish and uncooperative, but one of the reasons it is so successful is because it encourages people to do things that are deeply embedded in human nature. The awful thing about capitalism in the modern world is that it has resulted in some people having great power over other people. People have probably always exploited each other; modern capitalism allows them to do it on a massive scale.

My ideas did not go over well with the socialists. In fact the young man who spoke first even made fun of me a bit when he wrapped things up at the end of the discussion, saying that everyone knows that everything changed when people finally came down out of the trees. The one person at the meeting who seemed to know something about human evolution offered the idea that before the development of human civilizations (I took this to mean before the development of agriculture), the main conflict that early humans faced was that they were battling their environment to make a living, but everyone knows that humans were cooperative with each other.

Well, actually no one knows that. It is not inconceivable that this might have been the case, but again, if you consider how nonhuman primates behave, it seems unlikely that cooperation with *all* their fellow humans was a part of the life of our species before the advent of agriculture. If two species are closely related to each other, and each species has a particular trait, it is pretty likely that that trait was found in the common ancestor of those two species. It is quite often the case that monkeys and apes are greedy, selfish and uncooperative. It is quite often the case that humans are greedy, selfish and uncooperative. It is very likely the case that the common ancestor of all humans, monkeys and apes exhibited these traits as well.

On the other hand, people (and apes to be fair) while they are capable of some extraordinary awfulness, are also capable of self-sacrifice and general goodness. A close look at altruism in nonhuman primates suggests that when they are being generous, the recipients of that generosity tend to be individuals with whom they share genes. Or they are being generous because they are likely to have that generosity returned at a later date. Human generosity is not too dissimilar. If it were possible to quantify instances of human generosity, most of the time, like the other primates, humans would be observed being nice to their relatives first (blood is thicker than water), and then to individuals who might be of some use to them at a later date (you scratch my back, I'll scratch yours). But unlike the situation among the other primates, there is still a lot of altruism left in the human species after you subtract the generosity people display toward their relatives and others who can do them good in return.

From a sociobiological perspective, it is difficult to explain costly behaviors that provide no obvious benefits to the individuals who incur the cost. Not everything about human behavior can be explained by sociobiology. Nevertheless, I think it is only through a basic understanding of human nature as interpreted by that field that we can begin to get an idea of what people are about. The sociobiological paradigm is a powerful one. An understanding of evolution by natural selection, when added to some knowledge of the particular and peculiar history of the human species will go a long way towards an understanding of human behavior and human life in all its complexity. In an earlier chapter I suggested that feminists would do well to reconsider sociobiology because it is an essential starting point to understand the relations between the sexes. Similarly, I would suggest that people on the left should reconsider sociobiology and think hard about the circumstances that bring out the niceness in people.[2] How can altruism be encouraged among humans? How can the scale at which people are willing to cooperate be enlarged? How can people be convinced that people everywhere matter?

One message from sociobiology can be particularly useful here. That is that all humans are members of one species. Whatever our differences, each one of us bleeds red blood and has the same shared evolutionary legacy as every other member of the human species. The rules of evolution are relevant, if not the whole story, for people today. During the past 10,000 years much has changed for humans. Before the development of agriculture when the entire (rather small) human population lived by hunting and gathering, the world did not have the hierarchies that we do today. The complexities of living with six billion other people have developed rather recently. Individuals who lived by hunting and gathering were economic free agents, relying on themselves and their kin to collect the foods that they needed. Now, as we are reminded often, we are each a part of a global economy. And some people have vast power over others, politically, economically, and socially.

The evolutionary rule is that individual living things have been designed over the course of long periods of time to "maximize their reproduction." Many, many people, both straight and gay, break that rule in the modern world. In fact the idea that the maximization of reproduction is the goal of modern humans seems crazy. It isn't even a guideline, let alone a rule at this point in the human story. Many other desires guide human behavior in the modern world. Reproduction is one of many things that most people seem to want. So although sociobiology is useful, it certainly is not sufficient in itself for an understanding of human behavior in the twenty-first century. It has general relevance but falls short on specific topics. Homosexuality, for example, is clearly something that cannot be explained simply in terms of an evolutionary perspective.

The evolutionary hypotheses that have been suggested to explain how a gay gene might have been maintained in the human species are fairly weak. It is necessary to look at the bigger picture of the history of the human species in the past 10,000 years or so to come up with a plausible explanation for the existence of exclusive homosexuality, a feature of the human species that "shouldn't" have evolved according to the logic of natural selection. If there is a gay gene, it has survived in the human species because of human cultures and the particular demography of our species. If a gay gene first evolved in the human species after cultural rules were in place that prescribed marriage for all individuals in a social group, then a gay gene might have been carried along through generations whether or not the individuals who had that gene really wanted to have sex with their official spouses. It is a very recent development, from an evolutionary perspective, that all individuals are not being married off to suitable opposite-sex partners by the families into which they were born. Even a gay icon like Oscar Wilde (born in 1854) was married to a woman and fathered children.

The hundred years or so that elapsed from the late nineteenth century, when homosexuality was first named in the Western medical literature, to the end of the twentieth when gay people became a cultural force in America, is an evolutionary blink of an eye. When Foucault said that by acquiring a name, the homosexual became a species, he was not, of course, referring to a species in the biological sense. He was referring to the public birth of a *type* of person, a person who is sexually oriented towards other individuals of the same biological sex. It is curious that this type of person is considered by some to be a somewhat recent invention. It is interesting too, that there is very little evidence from the natural world that individual animals are exclusively homosexual. Animal species have no cultural rules proscribing exclusive homosexuality. Other species often exhibit homosexual *behavior* but it is very rare among free-living, naturally reproducing species to find individuals who are *exclusively* sexually oriented towards others of the same sex. If anything, nonhuman primates, for example, are best described as bisexual. Many people, including rather famously Sigmund Freud,[3] have suggested that humans are naturally bisexual as well. Bisexuality is less of an evolutionary conundrum than homosexuality because of the likelihood that reproduction is still occurring.

Is a human tendency towards bisexuality exploited by some cultures while being quashed in others? It is the case that some human groups expect that everyone can respond sexually to persons of both sexes. And in those cultures pretty much everyone does. In recent Western cultures however bisexuality seems, if this is possible, to be more reviled than homosexuality. And yet many people who otherwise believe themselves to be entirely straight can get in touch with their inner gay person if, for example, they find themselves in a sex-segregated setting like a prison. Behaviorally, it seems, many people can go either way. But, again, what people do and what people want are not always the same thing. Even in cultures like some of those seen in Melanesia where all males are expected to have sex with each other for a period of time, some participants are unenthusiastic about the practice and some take to it like the proverbial duck takes to water. It might be the case that human *behavior* is considerably more flexible than human *desire*. What people really want sexually might be something that is a core part of their beings. Rather than being "constructed," individuals might have an innate sexual desire for either males or females, even if their sexual behavior is more flexible and dependant upon circumstances.

Cultural anthropology can tell us very little about sexual desire among humans, but if it is the case that some people in every cultural group are oriented towards other individuals of the same sex, that could be seen as support for the idea that there is a gay gene in the human species. Again, lifelong exclusive homosexuality is a rare or even unknown phenomenon in many cultures, but it could nevertheless be the case that some individuals in every social group experience desire for individuals of the same biological sex. In some cultures in which the concept of homosexuality is unknown, that desire might go unnamed. It might or might not be acted upon. In recent Western cultures that desire is named and has been, officially, since the late nineteenth century. And many people have openly embraced the concept and the identity, especially in the later years of the twentieth century and the beginning of the twenty-first.

Although recent Western cultures are hardly an appropriate model for making statements about the human species, let's say, for argument's sake, that a small percentage of people in every human group are sexually oriented towards others of the same sex. Let's say, also for argument's sake, that these people have a gay gene and the "I was born this way" sentiment that so many gay people express is a reflection of a genetic difference between themselves and their heterosexual neighbors. Even though it seems to contradict natural selection, such a gene might have been maintained among humans because of the peculiar history of our species. But can that gene be maintained in the future if the people who have it are exempt from heterosexual marriage? Here's where things might start to get a bit tricky for the gay gene.

Fortunately, the gay gene is essentially just a metaphor. In real life, it seems quite unlikely that there is just *one* segment of DNA found within the human genome that somehow *determines* that the individuals who have that gene will be homosexually oriented. It seems extremely unlikely that every gay person alive today has that same DNA sequence. Even the gay gene study by Dean Hamer looked purposefully at a *subset* of the population of American gay men. Many gay men do not have the type of family tree that Hamer's pairs of gay brothers had. Sexual orientation of every variety is likely to be "caused" by a constellation of genes which interacts with a wide variety of environments in the development of human beings. To complicate things more, it also seems quite possible that different genes could be at the root of sexual orientation in men and women.

Furthermore, with six billion plus humans in the world today, if there are gay genes in the human genome, it is quite likely that there are many, many copies of those genes. And these genes are shared by the biological families of gay people, many of whom are themselves straight and reproducing. Again, if the gay gene study by Dean Hamer is valid, it is interesting that the gene in question was on the X chromosome because this chromosome is found twice as often in women as in men and there is no evidence that this particular gene results in homosexually oriented females. The survival of this "gay gene" would not seem to be in doubt.

Lifelong, exclusive homosexuality is an evolutionary conundrum, but many people experience shifts over time in their sexual orientation. It is quite possible that if there is a gay gene it will continue to survive in the human population because individuals who have it spend part of their lives as active heterosexuals. Active heterosexuality could lead to children and the continuing existence of gay genes. Many gay people have children from heterosexual relationships. Many other gay people have children through a variety of arrangements, including donor insemination, for example. If there is a gay gene it seems that it could be residing in the human genome in a separate place from genes that suggest to people that they might want to reproduce. Same-sex desire is separate from, but can co-exist happily with, a desire to pass along one's genes.

Although by the logic of evolutionary theory a gay gene should not exist, it is nevertheless possible that such genes are found in the human genome. Does this invalidate the entire field of sociobiology? No, it does not. What it says to me is that sociobiology is relevant to modern human lives but it isn't the entire story on human behavior. Homosexuality is an excellent illustration of why it is important to consider genes *and* environment, biology *and* culture, nature *and* nurture when discussing human behavior. Human behavior is complicated and develops from multiple, complex sources. Modern people both follow and refuse to follow the same evolutionary rules that other species live by. Sorting out what people do and do not have in common with other species is a big task, but it is a fine place to start if your goal is to understand what humans are about.

ENDNOTES

Notes to Chapter One

1. See J D'Emilio (1998) *Sexual Politics, Sexual Communities: The Making of a Homosexual Minority in the United States, 1940-1970*, 2nd edition (Chicago: University of Chicago Press; the first edition of this book was published in 1983, also by the University of Chicago Press). Also, L Faderman (1991) *Odd Girls and Twilight Lovers: A History of Lesbian Life in Twentieth-Century America* (NY: Columbia University Press).

2. J D'Emilio and EB Freedman (1988) *Intimate Matters: A History of Sexuality in America* (NY: Harper & Row), p. 320.

3. Faderman *Odd Girls* (note 1), p. 132. The American Psychiatric Association removed homosexuality from its list of mental disorders in 1973.

4. *Time*, April 14, 1997. There was a similar article in *Newsweek* on the same date.

5. AC Kinsey, WB Pomeroy and CE Martin (1948) *Sexual Behavior in the Human Male* (Philadelphia: WB Saunders). The companion volume on women was published in 1953 with the author listed as The Institute for Sex Research, Indiana University (*Sexual Behavior in the Human Female*, Philadelphia: WB Saunders).

6. Kinsey, et al. 1948, p. 651.

7. Ibid.

8. R Mestel (1994) "Sex by the Numbers" (*Discover* January 1994), p. 70.

9. DH Hamer, S Hu, VL Magnuson, N Hu, and A Pattatucci (1993) "A linkage between DNA markers on the X chromosome and male sexual orientation" (*Science* 261: 321-27).

10. RL Sell, JA Wells, and D Wypij (1995) "The prevalence of homosexual behavior and attraction in the United States, the United Kingdom and France: Results of national population-based samples" (*Archives of Sexual Behavior* 24(3), p. 235 (abstract). Specifically, this study found that "20.8, 16.3, and 18.5% of males, and 17.8, 18.6, and 18.5% of females in the

United States, the United Kingdom, and France report either homosexual behavior or homosexual attraction since age 15."

11. Cambridge MA: The Belknap Press of Harvard University Press 1975.
12. NY: Free Press.
13. SJ Gould (1994) "Curveball" (*The New Yorker* November 28, 1994), p. 147. Gould also wrote an excellent history of the misuse of biological information to support racism: *The Mismeasure of Man* (NY: WW Norton 1996; the first edition of this book was published in 1981, also by WW Norton).
14. R Boyd and JB Silk (1997) *How Humans Evolved* (NY: WW Norton), p. 559.

Notes to Chapter Two

1. NY: Picador USA/Farrar, Straus and Giroux 1998, p. 9.
2. Charles Darwin's *The Voyage of the Beagle* is available in a number of paperback editions including an abridged Penguin edition (1989). Darwin's "Journal of researches into the geology and natural history of the various countries visited by H.M.S. Beagle" was published after his return to England.
3. See, for example, D Lack *Darwin's Finches* (Cambridge: Cambridge University Press 1947), and more recently, J Weiner *The Beak of the Finch* (NY: Vintage 1995).
4. "The traditional universe was extremely short-lived since the six days of creation were supposed to have occurred only a few thousand years ago. In the seventeenth century, Archbishop James Ussher tried to calculate the date of creation by working back through the biblical patriarchs to Adam and fixed the year as 4004 B.C." PJ Bowler (1989) *Evolution: The History of an Idea*, revised ed. (Berkeley CA: University of California Press), p. 4.
5. There are many editions of *The Origin of Species*. I will be quoting here from the 1985 Penguin Classics edition. John Murray published the 1859 edition in London and the full title was *On the Origin of Species by Means of Natural Selection, or the Preservation of Favoured Races in the Struggle for Life.*
6. See PJ Bowler, Chapter Eleven "The Evolutionary Synthesis" (note 4).

7. "Hence, as more individuals are produced than can possibly survive, there must in every case be a struggle for existence …. It is the doctrine of Malthus applied with manifold force to the whole animal and vegetable kingdoms …." (*Origin*, p. 117). There is a Penguin Classics edition (1985) of Thomas Malthus's *An Essay on the Principle of Population*, which was originally published in 1798.

8. It has been suggested that embryos compete within their mother's uterus, and there is some empirical evidence to support that idea.

9. In a species that is neither expanding nor contracting, individuals will be replaced on a one-to-one basis in the next generation. Each average female will probably have one offspring to replace herself and one offspring to replace a male who is not giving birth directly himself.

10. Individuals of some species pursue an "r-strategy" in which speed of reproduction and a large quantity of offspring are favored. By contrast, "K-strategy" involves the production of a smaller number of offspring, each of which is more intensively nurtured. M Daly and M Wilson *Sex, Evolution, and Behavior*, 2nd ed. (Belmont CA: Wadsworth Publishing Co. 1983), pp. 199-202, referring to a paper by Robert MacArthur ("Some generalized theorems of natural selection," *Proc. Nat'l Acad. Sci. USA* 48: 1893-97 (1962)).

11. *The Descent of Man, and Selection in Relation to Sex* (Princeton NJ: Princeton University Press 1981). Originally published in London in 1871 by John Murray.

12. Ibid. There is also a large quantity of more recent empirical and theoretical research on this topic.

13. *Origin* (note 5), p. 458.

14. "Parental investment and sexual selection" in *Sexual Selection and the Descent of Man, 1871-1971*, ed. by B Campbell (Chicago: Aldine 1972) , pp. 136-179.

15. Primatologist Barbara Smuts has written a terrific paper on this topic called "The evolutionary origins of patriarchy" (*Human Nature* 6(1): 1-32, 1995).

Notes to Chapter Three

1. NY: Atlantic Monthly Press 1997.
2. UW Huck (1984) "Lemming migrations" in *The Encyclopedia of Mammals*, ed. by D Macdonald (NY: Facts on File), pp. 656-57.
3. RL Trivers (1971) "The evolution of reciprocal altruism" (*Quarterly Review of Biology* 46: 35-57).
4. WD Hamilton (1964) "The genetical evolution of social behaviour, I and II" (*Journal of Theoretical Biology* 7: 1-52).
5. See Chapter Eight "Reproductive Altruism" in Robert Trivers *Social Evolution* (Menlo Park CA: Benjamin/Cummings Publishing 1985), pp. 169-202. Page 177: "One of William Hamilton's greatest achievements was the discovery of an underlying genetic reason for the complex, female-based societies of the Hymenoptera (ants, bees, and wasps). The Hymenoptera are haplodiploid. That is, females have two sets of chromosomes, one from each parent, and are diploid, while males arise from *unfertilized* eggs and have only one set of chromosomes (they are haploid). This leads to a series of unusual degrees of relatedness …." (emphasis in original).
6. NY: Oxford University Press. A new edition of *The Selfish Gene* was published in 1989, also by Oxford University Press.
7. Ibid., p. ix (1976 edition).
8. M Daly and M Wilson (1983) *Sex, Evolution, and Behavior*, 2nd ed. (Belmont CA: Wadsworth Publishing Co.), p. 30. Trivers (note 5, pp. 46-47) discusses the significance of this jest and cites JBS Haldane (1955) "Population genetics" *New Biology* 18: 34-51.
9. See, for example, "The diet of Worms and the defenestration of Prague" *Natural History* 9/96.
10. SJ Gould and RC Lewontin (1984) "The spandrels of San Marco and the Panglossian paradigm: A critique of the adaptationist programme" in *Conceptual Issues in Evolutionary Biology*, ed. by E Sober (Cambridge MA: The MIT Press), pp. 252-70. Originally published in 1979: *Proc. R. Soc. Lond. B* 205: 581-98.
11. More specifically, Angier was referring to "hard-core evolutionary psychologists" in "Men, women, sex and Darwin" *The New York Times Magazine*, Feb. 21, 1999, p. 48.

12. A book could be written on this topic and indeed one has; see DE Brown (1991) *Human Universals* (NY: McGraw-Hill).
13. In a brief but wide-ranging paper, GJ Mihalik (1991) discusses the "us" vs. "them" mindset in the context of homosexuality as a stigmatized category ("From anthropology: Homosexuality, stigma, and biocultural evolution," *Journal of Gay & Lesbian Psychotherapy* 1(4): 15-29).

Notes to Chapter Four

1. F Rich "The sounds of silencing," *The New York Times* op-ed June 17, 2000, and J Rutenberg and S Elliott "Advertisers shun talk show as gay protest gains power," *The New York Times* May 19, 2000. In Schlessinger's own words, "We were biologically meant to give birth to more people. Not being able to relate normally to a member of the opposite sex is some kind of error. I do not see that as insulting at all. It is a statement of biological fact …. Some people just don't want to hear the truth" (*Time* July 3, 2000, pp. 59-60).
2. JC Mitani (1985) "Mating behavior of male orangutans in the Kutai Reserve, East Kalimantan, Indonesia" (*Animal Behavior* 33: 392-402).
3. RC Connor, RA Smolker and AF Richards (1992) "Two levels of alliance formation among male bottlenose dolphins (Tursiops sp.)" (*Proceedings of the National Academy of Science USA* 89: 987-90); also, RA Smolker, AF Richards, RC Connor and JW Pepper (1992) "Sex differences in patterns of association among Indian Ocean bottlenose dolphins" (*Behaviour* 123(1-2): 38-69).
4. BB Smuts and RW Smuts (1992) "Male aggression and sexual coercion of females in nonhuman primates and other mammals: Evidence and theoretical implications" in *Advances in the Study of Behavior*, vol. 22, pp. 1-63, ed. by PJB Slater, et al.; also BB Smuts (1992) "Male aggression against women: An evolutionary perspective" (*Human Nature* 3(1): 1-44).
5. *The Chimpanzees of Gombe: Patterns of Behavior* (Cambridge MA: Belknap/Harvard University Press 1986).
6. Ibid., p. 529.

7. T Struhsaker and L Leland (1987) "Colobines: Infanticide by adult males" in *Primate Societies*, ed. by B Smuts, et al. (Chicago: The University of Chicago Press), pp. 83-97.

8. Voltaire's Master Pangloss in *Candide* spoke of things always being for the best in this best of all possible worlds.

9. NY: St. Martin's Press 1999.

10. Ibid., pp. 16-17.

11. Ibid., pp. 25-26.

12. Ibid., p. 9.

13. Ibid., p. 290.

14. P Vasey (1999) "Review of Biological Exuberance" (*Animal Behaviour* 57: 223-24), p. 224.

15. P Vasey (1995) "Homosexual behavior in primates: A review of evidence and theory" (*International Journal of Primatology* 16(2): 173-204).

16. Ibid., p. 195.

17. Ibid., p. 177.

18. Ibid., p. 182.

19. Ibid., p. 173.

20. Ibid., p. 183.

21. See, for example, F De Waal and F Lanting (1997) *Bonobo: The Forgotten Ape* (Berkeley: University of California Press); T Kano (1992) *The Last Ape: Pygmy Chimpanzee Behavior and Ecology*, translated by Evelyn Ono Vineberg (Stanford CA: Stanford University Press); and references therein.

22. F De Waal (1995) "Bonobo sex and society" (*Scientific American* March 1995), p. 84.

23. Kano *The Last Ape* (note 21), pp. 190-191.

24. G Idani (1991) "Social relationships between immigrant and resident bonobo (*Pan paniscus*) females at Wamba" (*Folia Primatologica* 57: 83-95).

25. Some primatologists have an anecdote or two about specific pairs of same sex nonhuman primates who have been observed having sex with each other apparently to the detriment of their heterosexual options, but this is rarely mentioned in the literature.

26. Regarding Japanese macaque females in particular, Paul Vasey and Carole Gauthier state that these animals "are not preferentially heterosexual as commonly assumed .... Instead,

they are best characterized as bisexual" (p. 23). ("Skewed sex ratios and female homosexual activity in Japanese macaques: An experimental analysis" *Primates* 41(1): 17-25, 2000).

27. R Wrangham (1993) "The evolution of sexuality in chimpanzees and bonobos" (*Human Nature* 4(1): 47-79).
28. Ibid., pp. 65-66.
29. See references in note 4.

Notes to Chapter Five

1. NY: Alfred A. Knopf 1997, p. 129.
2. S LeVay (1991) "A difference in hypothalamic structure between heterosexual and homosexual men" (*Science* 253: 1034-37). LeVay's book on this topic, intended for general audiences, was published in 1993 (*The Sexual Brain*, Cambridge MA: The MIT Press).
3. LeVay "was rocketed from the hushed halls of the Salk Institute to the glare of *MacNeil/Lehrer*, *Oprah*, and *Donahue*. His work, career, and life were dissected on *Nightline* and in *Newsweek*" (D Nimmons "Sex and the brain" [*Discover*, March 1994], p. 68). See also N Angier "Zone of brain linked to men's sexual orientation" (*The New York Times*, August 30, 1991, pp. A1 & D18); C Gorman "Are gay men born that way?" (*Time*, September 9, 1991); R Massa "The way we wear our genes" (*The Village Voice*, December 24, 1991, p. 49).
4. P Gray (1991) *Psychology* (NY: Worth Publishers), p. 180, and AC Guyton (1976) *Structure and Function of the Nervous System*, 2nd ed. (Philadelphia PA: WB Saunders Co.), p. 205.
5. LeVay, *The Sexual Brain* (note 2), p. 120.
6. S LeVay and DH Hamer (1994) "Evidence for a biological influence in male homosexuality" (*Scientific American*, May 1994, pp. 44-49), p. 46.
7. Nimmons (note 3), p. 66.
8. LeVay, *The Sexual Brain* (note 2), pp. 120-121.
9. Ibid., p. 121.
10. W Byne, et al. (2001) "The interstitial nuclei of the human anterior hypothalamus: An investigation of variation with sex, sexual orientation, and HIV status" (*Hormones and Behavior* 40: 86-92), p. 86.

11. See "Biology behind homosexuality in sheep, study confirms," press release dated March 5, 2004 from the Oregon Health & Science University (www.ohsu.edu/news/), discussing research by CE Roselli et al., published in *Endocrinology*, February 2004.

12. DF Swaab and MA Hofman (1990) "An enlarged suprachiasmatic nucleus in homosexual men" (*Brain Research* 537: 141-148; the suprachiasmatic nucleus is 1.7 times larger in gay men than straight men). LS Allen and RA Gorski (1992) "Sexual orientation and the size of the anterior commissure in the human brain" (*Proc. Nat'l Acad. Sci. USA* 89: 7199-7202; women have a larger anterior commissure than straight men, and gay men have a larger anterior commissure than women).

13. JM Bailey and RC Pillard (1991) "A genetic study of male sexual orientation" (*Arch. Gen. Psychiatry* 48: 1089-1096). See also news coverage of the study in *Science*, "Twin study links genes to homosexuality," C Holden, Jan. 3, 1992, p. 33.

14. JM Bailey, RC Pillard, MC Neale, and Y Agyei (1993) "Heritable factors influence sexual orientation in women" (*Arch. Gen. Psychiatry* 50: 217-223). See also news coverage of the study in *The New York Times*, "Study suggests genes sway lesbians' sexual orientation," N Angier, Mar. 12, 1993.

15. See "Double Mystery" by L Wright (*The New Yorker*, Aug. 7, 1995) for an interesting discussion of research on twins.

16. See FL Whitam, M Diamond and J Martin (1993) "Homosexual orientation in twins: A report on 61 pairs and three triplet sets" (*Archives of Sexual Behavior* 22(3): 187-206), and discussion of similar studies therein.

17. RC Pillard, J Poumadere and RA Carretta (1981) "Is homosexuality familial? A review, some data, and a suggestion" (*Archives of Sexual Behavior* 10(5): 465-75); JM Bailey and DS Benishay (1993) "Familial aggregation of female sexual orientation" (*Am. J. Psychiatry* 150(2): 272-77); JM Bailey and AP Bell (1993) "Familiality of female and male homosexuality" (*Behavior Genetics* 23(4): 313-22).

18. DH Hamer, S Hu, VL Magnuson, N Hu, and A Pattatucci (1993) "A linkage between DNA markers on the X chromosome and male sexual orientation" (*Science* 261: 321-27). The paper is reproduced as Appendix A in a book for a popular audience

that was published in 1994 by Hamer and co-author Peter Copeland (*The Science of Desire: The Search for the Gay Gene and the Biology of Behavior* [NY: Simon & Schuster]).

19. See, for example, *The New York Times* ("Report suggests homosexuality is linked to genes," by N Angier, pp. A1, A12, July 16, 1993); and *The Economist* ("A gay gene?" unsigned article, p. 80, July 17, 1993) as well as discussion of media response to the study detailed by Hamer in *The Science of Desire* (note 18). Among other things, Hamer appeared on *Nightline* to discuss this research.

20. See Letter on "Genetics and male sexual orientation" by A Fausto-Sterling and E Balaban (*Science*, 261: 1257 [1993]).

21. Hamer et al. (note 18, 1993), p. 323.

22. Ibid., p. 322.

23. Ibid., p. 321.

24. S Hu, et al. (1995) "Linkage between sexual orientation and chromosome Xq28 in males but not in females" (*Nature Genetics*, 11: 248-56). See also "New evidence of a 'gay gene,'" by A Toufexis in *Time*, Nov. 13, 1995, p. 95.

25. G Rice, C Anderson, N Risch, and G Ebers (1999) "Male homosexuality: Absence of linkage to microsatellite markers at Xq28" (*Science* 284: 665-67). See also, "Study questions gene influence on male homosexuality," E Goode, *The New York Times*, Apr. 23, 1999.

26. KI Mills (1994) "Study finds link between fingerprints and male homosexuality" (*Ann Arbor News*, Dec. 26, 1994, p. A7), reporting on JA Hall and D Kimura (1994) "Dermatoglyphic asymmetry and sexual orientation in men" (*Behavioral Neuroscience* 108(6): 1203-06).

27. Mills (note 26).

28. D McFadden and EG Pasanen (1998) "Comparison of the auditory systems of heterosexuals and homosexuals: Click-evoked otoacoustic emissions" (*Proc. Nat'l Acad. Sci. USA* 95: 2709-13), and wire service coverage from Reuters and Associated Press on Mar. 3, 1998.

29. SM Breedlove, et al. (2000) "Finger-length ratios and sexual orientation" (*Nature* 404: 455-56).

30. I Savic, H Berglund and P Lindstrom (2005) "Brain response to putative pheromones in homosexual men" (*Proceedings of the National Academy of Sciences* 102(20): 7356-61).

31. Ibid., p. 7356.

32. R Mestel, "X marks the spot" (*Discover*, Jan. 1994, p. 71).

33. J Lever (1994) "Sexual revelations" (*The Advocate* Aug. 23, 1994, p. 20).

34. J Lever (1995) "Lesbian sex survey" (*The Advocate* Aug. 22, 1995, pp. 28-29).

35. J Schmalz (1993) "Poll finds an even split on homosexuality's cause," *The New York Times*, Mar. 5, 1993, p. A14; DW Moore (1993) "Public polarized on gay issue" (*Gallup Poll Monthly*, Apr. 1993, p. 30: the group of people polled who say that homosexuality is "'something that people are born with' … displays the most tolerant attitudes towards gays"); A Yang (1999) "From wrongs to rights," a publication of The Policy Institute of the National Gay and Lesbian Task Force, p. 19, and references therein.

36. LeVay, *The Sexual Brain* (note 2), p. 1.

37. N Angier (note 14).

38. C Holden (note 13).

Notes to Chapter Six

1. NY: Alfred A. Knopf, 2000, pp. 4-5.

2. See ER Wolf (1982) *Europe and the People without History* (Berkeley CA: University of California Press).

3. See three papers published simultaneously in 1991 in *Soc. Sci. Med.* 33(8): "Anthropology rediscovers sex: Introduction," by S Lindenbaum (pp. 865-66); "Sex, culture and the anthropologist," by D Tuzin (pp. 867-74); and "Anthropology rediscovers sexuality: A theoretical comment," by CS Vance (pp. 875-84).

4. NY: Harcourt Brace.

5. Ibid., p. 453.

6. Ibid., p. 584.

7. Apparently he did; see pages 472-73 of *The Sexual Life of Savages* (note 4).

8. JM Carrier (1980) "Homosexual behavior in cross-cultural perspective." In *Homosexual Behavior: A Modern Reappraisal*, ed. by J Marmor (NY: Basic Books, pp. 100-22), pp. 101-102, quoting F Williams 1936, *Papuans of the Trans-Fly* (London: Oxford University Press). In 1977 TK Fitzgerald said that *Papuans of the Trans-Fly* "still constitutes one of the best coverages of institutionalized homosexual behavior we have" ("A critique of anthropological research on homosexuality" *J. Homo.* 2(4): 385-97), p. 392.

9. K Weston (1993) "Lesbian/gay studies in the house of anthropology" (*Ann. Rev. Anthropol.* 22: 339-67), p. 346. Weston also mentions influential anthropologists Ruth Benedict and Alfred Kroeber as having a similar perspective. See also, G Herdt (1991) on George Devereux in "Representations of homosexuality: An essay on cultural ontology and historical comparison, part I" (*Journal of the History of Sexuality* 1(3): 481-504), pp. 489ff.

10. Weston (note 9), p. 339. This review contains a good summary of this subject.

11. Fitzgerald (note 8), p. 389. Like the Weston review, a good summary of anthropology and homosexuality.

12. D Sonenschein (1966) "Homosexuality as a subject of anthropological inquiry" (*Anthropological Quarterly* 39(2): 73-82), p. 75.

13. Fitzgerald (note 8), p. 385.

14. *American Anthropologist* 72: 1428-34 (1970).

15. Fitzgerald (note 8), p. 391.

16. E Blackwood and SE Wieringa (1999) "Sapphic shadows: Challenging the silence in the study of sexuality" in *Female Desires: Same-Sex Relations and Transgender Practices Across Cultures*, ed. by E Blackwood and SE Wieringa (NY: Columbia University Press, pp. 39-63), p. 40.

17. "The homosexual role," *Social Problems* 16: 182-92 (1968).

18. Ibid., p. 182.

19. Ibid., p. 187.

20. JD Weinrich and WL Williams (1991) "Strange customs, familiar lives: Homosexualities in other cultures," in *Homosexuality: Research Implications for Public Policy*, ed. by JC Gonsoriek and

J Weinrich (Newbury Park CA: Sage Publications, pp. 44-59), p. 47.

21. B Risman and P Schwartz (1988) "Sociological research on male and female homosexuality" (*Ann. Rev. Sociol.* 14: 125-47), p. 130.

22. *History of Sexuality, Volume I: An Introduction* (NY: Vintage Books 1980; originally published in French in 1976 by Editions Gallimard), p. 37.

23. Ibid., p. 43.

24. See Weston (note 9), p. 341 and Weinrich and Williams (note 20), p. 47. Per SO Murray, "It is not only in the modern West that some persons have noticed same-sex sexual desires .... I consider it incredibly arrogant – specifically chronocentric and ethnocentric – to proclaim that no one recognized homosexual desires before late-nineteenth-century forensic psychiatrists wrote about it" (*Homosexualities*, Chicago: The University of Chicago Press 2000, p. 8).

25. R Mendes-Leite (1993) "On the esthetics of pleasures: Guidelines for a socio-anthropology of (homo)sexualities" (*J. Homo.* 1993 25(1/2): 17-30), p. 25.

26. JD DeLamater and JS Hyde (1998) "Essentialism vs. social constructionism in the study of human sexuality" (*The Journal of Sex Research* 35(1): 10-18), p. 10.

27. See, for example, FL Whitam (1987) "A cross-cultural perspective on homosexuality, transvestism and trans-sexualism," in *Variant Sexuality: Research and Theory,* ed. by GD Wilson (Baltimore MD: Johns Hopkins University Press, pp. 176-201). P. 176: "The predictable, universal appearance of homosexual persons, despite socialisation into heterosexual patterns of behaviour suggests not only that homosexual orientation is biologically based but that sexual orientation itself is also biologically derived." Pp. 198-99: "Homosexual men and lesbians probably appear in all or nearly all societies."

28. Influential social constructionist Jeffrey Weeks was himself quite clear about this distinction going back to 1981 (*Sex Politics and Society*, NY: Longman, p. 96), but nonetheless confusion continues. See also McIntosh (note 17), p. 187.

29. Weston (note 9), p. 341.

30. Vance (note 3), p. 878.

31. Ibid.
32. Ibid.
33. Ibid.
34. For Western lesbian and gay history, see works by JN Katz, L Federman, J Boswell, and D Greenberg, among others.
35. 1952, Harper & Brothers.
36. Ibid., p. 130.
37. Ibid., p. 129.
38. Ibid., p. 143.
39. R Crapo (1995) "Factors in the cross-cultural patterning of male homosexuality: A reappraisal of the literature" (*Cross-Cultural Research* 29(2): 178-202), p. 179.
40. D Davis and R Whitten (1987) "The cross-cultural study of human sexuality" (*Ann. Rev. Anthropol.* 16: 69-98), p. 87 ("Researchers ... have typically sacrificed breadth of coverage for depth of analysis"), and R Bolton (1994) "Sex, science, and social responsibility: Cross-cultural research on same-sex eroticism and sexual intolerance" (*Cross-Cultural Research* 28(2): 134-90), p. 146 ("The recent ferment in ethnographic work on homosexualities is not matched by equal fervor among comparativists ...."). Bolton was however able to locate a dozen studies on the topic of same-sex eroticism, including the classic by Ford and Beach.
41. Boulder CO: Westview Press/HarperCollins.
42. Ibid., p. 7.
43. Ibid., p. 13.
44. Ibid., p. 61.
45. NY: Columbia University Press. Blackwood also edited another volume of cross-cultural studies of same-sex eroticism that was published in 1986 (*The Many Faces of Homosexuality*, NY: Harrington Park Press).
46. Chicago: University of Chicago Press, 2000.
47. Murray's categories are "age-structured homosexualities," "gender-stratified organization of homosexuality," and "egalitarian homosexualities."
48. Crapo (note 39, p. 184) refers to G Gorer's typology from 1966 which was discussed in *The Danger of Equality* (London: Cresset). Also often referred to is B Adam's (1986) typology "Age, structure, and sexuality: Reflections on the anthropological evidence on homosexual relations," in Blackwood, ed. (note 45),

pp. 19-33. See also D Greenberg's influential *The Construction of Homosexuality* (Chicago: University of Chicago Press 1988).

49. Blackwood and Wieringa (note 16), p. 46.
50. Davis and Whitten (note 40), p. 80.
51. Fitzgerald (note 8), p. 390.
52. Carrier (note 8), p. 118.
53. N Barber (1998) "Ecological and psychosocial correlates of male homosexuality: A cross-cultural investigation" (*Journal of Cross-Cultural Psychology* 29(3): 387-401).

Notes to Chapter Seven

1. Austin TX: University of Texas Press, p. 14.
2. In *Blood, Bread, and Poetry: Selected Prose 1979-1985* (NY: WW Norton, 1986, pp. 23-75). A note on page 23 reviews the publishing history of this essay.
3. Ibid., p. 35.
4. Ibid., p. 23.
5. Ibid., p. 32.
6. See two papers by BB Smuts: "The evolutionary origins of patriarchy" (*Human Nature* 6(1): 1-32, 1995); and "Male aggression against women: An evolutionary perspective" (*Human Nature* 3(1): 1-44, 1992).
7. See DE Brown (1991) *Human Universals* (NY: McGraw-Hill), and references therein.
8. G Herdt (1997) *Same Sex, Different Cultures: Gays and Lesbians Across Cultures* (Boulder CO: Westview Press/HarperCollins), pp. 67-69.
9. D Greenberg (1988) *The Construction of Homosexuality* (Chicago: The University of Chicago Press), p. 142.
10. *Homosexualities*, Chicago: The University of Chicago Press, 2000, p. 39.
11. Ibid., p. 40.
12. Ibid., p. 42. Murray is quoting Plutarch's essay on Pelopidas.
13. Herdt (note 8), p. 6 and Greenberg (note 9), p. 143.
14. Greenberg (note 9), pp. 143-44.
15. Ibid., p. 145.
16. As SO Murray notes, presumably one's "other half" is the same age (note 10, pp. 206 and 374). I would add that bisexuality

does not seem to be a viable option in this schema – presumably individuals have only one other half and thus should not logically be attracted to both men and women. This is rather ironic considering the men of ancient Greece would likely be considered to be bisexual in our terms.

17. KJ Dover *Greek Homosexuality* (1989 NY: MJF Books), p. 62, quoting Plato's *Symposium*.
18. G Herdt (note 8), p. 82; G Herdt "Representations of homosexuality: An essay on cultural ontology and historical comparison, part II" (*Journal of the History of Sexuality* 1991, 1(4): 603-32), p. 608; and Greenberg (note 9), p. 27.
19. G Herdt, introduction to the paperback edition of *Ritualized Homosexuality in Melanesia* (Berkeley CA: University of California Press 1984/1993), p. ix, citing Herdt 1991 (note 18).
20. Murray (note 10), p. 30.
21. I would say that Herdt's work is seminal but that would be a dreadful pun. On the Sambia, see G Herdt (1981) *Guardians of the Flutes: Idioms of Masculinity* (NY: McGraw-Hill), Herdt (note 8), and chapters in *Ritualized Homosexuality in Melanesia* (note 19). *Ritualized Homosexuality* is an edited volume that contains papers by others who have worked in this area; for other references, see Greenberg (note 9), p. 27fn.
22. Herdt (note 8), p. xiii.
23. RJ Stoller and G Herdt (1985) "Theories of origins of male homosexuality" (*Arch. Gen. Psychiatry* 42: 399-404), p. 400.
24. Herdt (note 18, 1991), p. 612.
25. Herdt, (note 8), p. 114, and Stoller and Herdt (note 23), p. 400.
26. Herdt, (note 18, 1991), p. 611.
27. Stoller and Herdt (note 23).
28. Ibid., p. 402.
29. Ibid.
30. Herdt (note 8), p. 121.
31. Herdt (note 19, 1984/1993), p. xxxii.
32. G Herdt (1990) "Developmental discontinuities and sexual orientation across cultures," in *Homosexuality/Heterosexuality: Concepts of Sexual Orientation*, ed. by DP McWhirter, et al. (NY: Oxford University Press, pp. 208-36), p. 221.

33. W Roscoe (1998) *Changing Ones: Third and Fourth Genders in Native North America* (NY: St. Martin's Griffin), p. 10. See also Roscoe pp. 206-7 and Murray (note 10), pp. 350-51.

34. See discussion in Roscoe (note 33), pp. 17-19 and Murray (note 10), pp. 348-49, fn 74.

35. Roscoe (note 33), p. 7.

36. Ibid., p. 11.

37. Ibid., p. 8.

38. WL Williams (1986/1992) *The Spirit and the Flesh: Sexual Diversity in American Indian Culture* (Boston MA: Beacon Press), pp. 49-50.

39. Williams (note 38), p. 42.

40. Roscoe (note 33), pp. 27-28, quoting Osh-Tisch, a *boté* or Crow third gender person.

41. See Chapter Five of Roscoe (note 33).

42. Roscoe (note 33), p. 207.

43. E Blackwood (1998) "Tombois in West Sumatra: Constructing masculinity and erotic desire" (*Cultural Anthropology* 13(4): 491-521), p. 500.

44. B Risman and P Schwartz (1988) "Sociological research on male and female homosexuality" (*Ann. Rev. Sociol.* 14: 125-47), p. 143.

Notes to Chapter Eight

1. *In Search of Lost Time*, volume 5, translated by CKS Moncrieff and T Kilmartin, revised by DJ Enright, NY: Modern Library 1993, p. 408.

2. While a number of people may have expressed this opinion, Laura Howard first expressed it to me with complete clarity.

3. EF Keller (2000) *The Century of the Gene* (Cambridge MA: Harvard University Press), p. 74.

4. Ibid., p. 95.

5. In this paragraph, I am quoting from the *Advocate's* online version of the story "Sixteen Gay Lives," which is an expanded version of the *Advocate's* "Why Are We Gay?" printed edition cover story from July 17, 2001.

6. See discussion in Chapter Five, and references therein.

7. For example: "Even the most cursory examination of cultural and historical variation suggests that it is preposterous to imagine that what we in the modern West now conceptualize as homosexuality is innate." V Whisman, *Queer by Choice: Lesbians, Gay Men, and the Politics of Identity* (NY: Routledge 1996), p. 126.

8. See JD Weinrich (1987) "A new sociobiological theory of homosexuality applicable to societies with universal marriage" (*Ethology and Sociobiology* 8: 37-47). This paper also will be discussed later in this chapter.

9. I realize that another implication of this line of reasoning is that gay genes might die out if gay people are exempt from heterosexual marriage. The future of gay genes will be discussed in Chapter Nine.

10. For an alternative view of the possibility that homosexuality has evolved because groups are the locus for selection in evolution, see J Kirby (2003) "A new group-selection model for the evolution of homosexuality" (*Biology and Philosophy* 18: 683-694).

11. GE Hutchinson (1959) "A speculative consideration of certain possible forms of sexual selection in man" (*American Naturalist* 93: 81-91). Cited and discussed in JA Kirsch and JE Rodman (1982) "Selection and sexuality: The Darwinian view of homosexuality" in *Homosexuality: Social, Psychological and Biological Issues*, ed. by W Paul, et al. (Beverly Hills CA: Sage Publications, pp. 183-95) and Weinrich (note 8), p. 38. As Weinrich notes, although Hutchinson was "writing in the presociobiological era, [he] used what amounted to sociobiological logic .… "

12. Hutchinson (note 11), pp. 81-82.

13. R Boyd and JB Silk (1997) *How Humans Evolved* (NY: WW Norton), p. 538.

14. Ibid., p. 539.

15. Wilson attributed this idea to HT Spieth and RL Trivers (Cambridge MA: Belknap/Harvard University Press 1975), p. 555.

16. Ibid.

17. JR Krebs and NB Davies (1993) *An Introduction to Behavioural Ecology*, 3rd edition (Cambridge MA: Blackwell Scientific), p. 318.

18. Ibid., Chapter Twelve, pages 291-317.

19. D Bobrow and JM Bailey (2001) "Is male homosexuality maintained via kin selection?" (*Evolution and Human Behavior* 22: 361-68), p. 363.

20. Ibid., p. 361.

21. "Even if there are genes which, in today's environment, produce a homosexual phenotype, this does not mean that in another environment, say that of our Pleistocene ancestors, they would have had the same phenotypic effect. A gene for homosexuality in our modern environment might have been a gene for something utterly different in the Pleistocene .... It may be that the phenotype which we are trying to explain did not even exist in some earlier environment, even though the gene did then exist." Richard Dawkins (1982) *The Extended Phenotype* (NY: Oxford University Press), p. 38. (A phenotype is the physical manifestation of a genotype – which itself is the genetic make up of an individual. The Pleistocene was the prehistorical epoch going back to approximately 1½ million years ago.)

22. N Barber (1998) "Ecological and psychosocial correlates of male homosexuality: A cross-cultural investigation" (*Journal of Cross-Cultural Psychology* 29(3): 387-401).

23. *American Zoologist* 14: 249-64 (1974). RL Trivers was also discussed in Chapters Two and Three.

24. E Stein (1999) *The Mismeasure of Desire: The Science, Theory, and Ethics of Sexual Orientation* (NY: Oxford University Press), p. 233.

25. Weinrich (note 8).

26. Ibid., p. 37.

27. Ibid.

28. J McKnight (1997) *Straight Science? Homosexuality, Evolution and Adaptation* (NY: Routledge).

29. Ibid., p. 76.

30. Ibid., p. 106.

31. Ibid.

32. Ibid., p. 186.

33. Kirby (note 10), p. 687.

34. F Muscarella (2000) "The evolution of homoerotic behavior in humans" (*Journal of Homosexuality* 40(1): 51-77), p. 53. See also, F Muscarella (1999) "The homoerotic behavior that never evolved" (*Journal of Homosexuality* 37(3): 1-18).

35. RC Kirkpatrick (2000) "The evolution of human homosexual behavior" (*Current Anthropology* 41(3): 385-413).

36. This was discussed at the beginning of Chapter Three.

37. Kirkpatrick (note 35), p. 385.

38. D Hamer and P Copeland (1994) *The Science of Desire* (NY: Simon & Schuster, pp. 183-84), citing RL Trivers and W Rice. Summarized also by Kirby (note 10), p. 687.

39. A summary article is available at http://news.nature.com//news/2004/041011/041011-5.html, citing A Camperio-Ciani, F Corna and C Capiluppi (*Proc. R. Soc. Lond. B*, published online, doi:10.1098/rspb (2004)).

40. Weinrich (note 8), p. 43.

41. Less hypothetically, on the berdache tradition among Native Americans: "In small groups, with populations of a few hundred, there might have been only one or two berdaches in a given generation. In larger communities, their numbers were sufficient for them to be recognized as a social group." W Roscoe (1998) *Changing Ones: Third and Fourth Genders in Native North America* (NY: St. Martin's/Griffin), p. 11.

42. The human population at the end of the geological period known as the Pleistocene has been estimated to have been 3-10 million people (MN Cohen "Speculations on the evolution of density measurement and population regulation in *Homo sapiens*," p. 276 in *Biosocial Mechanisms of Population Regulation*, ed. by MN Cohen, et al., New Haven CT: Yale University Press, 1980). If the world was "saturated" with hunter-gatherers 10,000 years ago, the human population would only have been 15 million (J Landers "Reconstructing ancient populations" in *The Cambridge Encyclopedia of Human Evolution*, ed. by S Jones, et al., NY: Cambridge University Press 1992, pp. 402-405), p. 402.

43. Landers (note 42), p. 405.

44. Two relevant quotes: "Constructionists view sexuality as the result of complex, diffuse experiences. Partner preferences result from idiosyncratic personality requirements, socially structured opportunities, and cultural norms. Plummer ... and Weeks ... suggest that the very possibility for homosexuality to become a master status is the result of urbanization and industrialization. Freed from compulsory family membership by the possibility

of productive labor outside their kin group, men at least could seek identities from their personally chosen relationships." B. Risman and P. Schwartz (1988) "Sociological research on male and female homosexuality" (*Ann. Rev. Sociol.* 14: 125-47), p. 130.

"It is when a particular type of sex partner is rare in the society as a whole that the search costs for that type of sex will be most strongly influenced by urbanization .... By facilitating the creation of markets for homosexual activity, urbanization affects not only the geographic distribution of such activity but also its amount .... The total number of practicing homosexuals in a society will ... increase with the rise of cities, making homosexuality seem, and in a valid if partial sense be, a by-product of economic development and modernity." RA Posner (1992) *Sex and Reason* (Cambridge MA: Harvard University Press), pp. 126-27.

Notes to Chapter Nine

1. *Literary Reminiscences*, translated by David Magarshack (Chicago: Ivan R. Dee, Publisher), p. 135.
2. For example, people on the left sometimes criticize the concept of ownership of private property by individuals. I would suggest though that an interest in owning things (property in particular) is a part of human nature. Many primates are territorial – they "own" the land on which they live – and they will fight off other primates that encroach on their turf. This concept has a long history in the human lineage. Instead of suggesting that private property is bad, people on the left should consider switching their focus to a more equitable distribution of property. Rather than no one owning anything, it would be better from the perspective of human nature if everyone owned something.
3. S Freud (1930/1961) *Civilization and Its Discontents* (translated by James Strachey, NY: WW Norton), p. 61, footnote 7: "Man is an animal organism with (like others) an unmistakably bisexual disposition."

INDEX

A

Advocate, The (magazine) 93, 135
agriculture, development of 145, 154, 160, 162
AIDS 4, 82
altruism 38, 40, 42–43, 147, 149, 161–162
Ancient Greece 121–123
artificial selection 22

B

Bagemihl, Bruce 66–67
Bailey, J. Michael 83, 94
behavioral genetics 83–84, 86
berdache 126–128
bisexuality 73, 95, 164
Blackwood, Evelyn 111, 130
bonobos 69–71
boy-inseminating rites 124

C

capitalism 24, 56, 159–160
chimpanzees 12, 51, 55, 60–62, 70, 74, 153
coming out 4, 115, 119, 156
communication sex 74
communism 56
compulsory heterosexuality 117
costs and benefits 45, 76
cultural anthropology 16, 98–104, 109

D

Darwin, Charles 18–22, 29, 45
Dawkins, Richard 44–45
DeGeneres, Ellen 5, 115
de Lamarck, Jean Baptiste 20
demography 139, 152–156, 163
DNA 22, 40–44, 60, 63, 78, 80, 83–84, 86–88, 94–95, 133–134, 144, 166
DNA studies 86–88
domesticated animals 21–22

E

egalitarian homosexuality 112, 120, 126
essentialism 106, 130, 155
Evans-Pritchard, E.E. 104–105

F

female mate choice 30
feminism 34–36, 117, 162
Fitzgerald, Thomas 104
foragers. *See* hunter-gatherers
Ford, Clellan and Frank Beach 110
Foucault, Michel 105–107, 163
Freud, Sigmund 146, 164

G

Galapagos Islands 19–20
genito-genital rubbing (bonobos) 70

gibbons 51, 67, 69
Goodall, Jane 61, 68–69
gorillas 12, 51, 55, 60, 62, 69
Gould, Stephen Jay 11, 47

H

Hamer, Dean 6, 86–88, 92–95, 149, 166
Hamilton, W.D. 42, 44–45
helper at the nest 143–144
Herdt, Gilbert 111, 124
heterosexual marriage 120, 137–138, 147, 153
heterozygote advantage 141–142, 147
H.M.S. *Beagle* 19
Homo sapiens 8, 12, 60, 73, 139, 145
homosexuality, prevalence of 5–6, 85, 87
human nature xii, 16, 50, 52, 55–56, 97, 159–161
hunter-gatherers 113, 145
Hutchinson, G.E. 140, 142
hypothalamus 80–83, 94–95

I

INAH3 81–82
inclusive fitness 40, 42, 44
individual reproduction 140, 147, 152
infant mortality 26

K

Keller, Evelyn Fox 134
kin selection 9–10, 42–43, 142–147, 151

Kinsey, Alfred 5
Kirkpatrick, R.C. 149

L

lemmings 38–39
LeVay, Simon 80–83, 93–94, 95
Locke, John 57

M

male-male competition 30–31
Malinowski, Bronislaw 101–102
Malthus, Thomas 22
"maximizing" reproduction xi, 8, 48–49, 52, 162
McIntosh, Mary 105
McKnight, Jim 147–148
Mead, Margaret 101, 103, 114
Melanesia 120, 123–126, 164
Mendel, Gregor 22
modern synthesis 22
Murray, Stephen O. 111–112, 122
Muscarella, F. 148

N

"natural" behavior 59–63
natural history 15, 18
natural selection 8, 17–24, 29, 37–39, 42, 45, 47–48, 119, 140, 152, 156, 161, 163, 165
neuroanatomical studies 80–83
nonhuman primates 45, 59, 62, 67–69, 72–75, 77–78, 105, 117, 160–161, 164

nonhuman primates, homosexual behavior in 67–69, 72–75, 77–78, 105, 117, 164

North American Indians 126–127

O

orangutans 60–62, 69
Origin of Species, The (book title) 21, 32

P

parental investment 33–34, 36–37
parental manipulation 146
parent-offspring conflict 146
participant-observation 98–99
Pillard, Richard 83–85
population density 153
postmodernism 99–100
Pride parade 1–2
primates 8, 12, 27–28, 31, 38, 40, 45–46, 51, 55, 58–60, 62, 67–69, 72–75, 77–78, 105, 117, 160–161, 164

R

race 11–12, 56, 97
reciprocal altruism 40, 149
Rich, Adrienne 117–118
Roscoe, Will 128, 130

S

Sambia (Melanesia) 120, 123–126, 164

Schlessinger, Laura 59
sex differences 32, 34–35, 37, 51
sexual selection 18, 29–32
social constructionism 105–110, 155
social insects 43, 143–144
Sociobiology (book title) 9–10, 142
Sonenschein, David 104
Stein, Gertrude 115–116
Stonewall 2, 4
struggle for existence 23, 28–29
Symposium, The (Plato) 123, 129

T

tabula rasa 15, 17, 57
transgendered homosexuality 112, 120–121, 127
transgenerational homosexuality 112, 120–121, 124
Trivers, Robert 32, 36–37, 40, 45, 146, 149
twins 84–85, 95
two-spirit traditions 127
typologies 120

V

Vance, Carole 107–108
variation 22–23
Vasey, Paul 68–69

W

Wallace, Alfred Russel 21

Weinrich, James 146–147
Weston, Kath 104
Wilde, Oscar 163
Wilson, E.O. 9, 45, 142, 146
Wrangham, Richard 74

X

X-linked traits 149–150
Xq28 88, 94–95

ABOUT THE AUTHOR

N. J. Peters is a freelance writer and editor who lives in New York City. Contact: conundrumbook@earthlink.net.